If you have ever wondered, *"How can this be my life?"* and, *"Is God really in the midst of this?"* you have got to read this book! Each page of *Cancer on Monday, Dead on Tuesday, Home by the Weekend* brings hope and inspiration. A true keeper!

—Sheila Karsevar
Wellness Coach

This book provoked in me a new awareness of all that God orchestrates for us among the twists and turns that we encounter in our daily lives. A story about the power of relationship, faith, and love, *Cancer on Monday, Dead on Tuesday, Home by the Weekend* helps us to notice a grander plan with "small wonders sprinkled everywhere."

—Kim Bowers-Antioch
Provider Relations Specialist

So many people wonder if God really exists, and if He does exist, how involved is He in our lives? Do the miracles we read about in the Bible still happen today? Tricia's true story reveals the answers to those questions. Yes! God exists. And He is intimately involved in our lives in so many ways—ways we see in the moment and ways we only recognize as we look back and reflect on where life has led us and how we got there. And sometimes, in ways we will never know or understand. Do miracles still happen today? Absolutely! The miracle of new life when it seemed a healthy birth was no longer possible. The miracle of a life saved when death seemed to have a strong grip on her mother, and the miracle of her mom's complete healing from cancer. So be encouraged as you read one more testimony to the fact that God exists, and He loves you so much and He is intimately involved in your life in both the little details and the big miracles!

—Rev. James R. Dries
Senior Pastor, First Baptist Church, Milton, Pennsylvania

Cancer on Monday, Dead on Tuesday, Home by the Weekend is a must read! Tricia Pawling-King never lost faith in the face of tragedy and shows us how things that happen to you in life are not coincidences. This miraculous book takes you on a truly inspirational journey that will make you want to read it again and again.

—Amanda Petrak
Public Relations at Key Bank

CANCER
ON MONDAY,
DEAD
ON TUESDAY,
HOME
BY THE WEEKEND

FINDING HOPE IN THE STORM

TRICIA PAWLING KING

5 Fold Media
Visit us at www.5foldmedia.com

This is for you, Mom, with love overflowing.

Acknowledgements

What started as a simple journal took on a life of its own and has taken me on a path I could have never foreseen. It brought me here, having a book published that I never intended to write. But now that we are at this point, my heart overflows with gratitude for how we got there.

My deepest and most sincere thanks goes to:

God, for saving my mother from the depths of darkness and bringing her back to us and for all the amazing blessings you have provided in my life. For the night You kept me awake, showing me so clearly what I needed to do, and giving me the strength to see this project through to the end that it may touch the lives of others.

My husband Charles, my love for you is beyond words that can be put on paper. Your tireless support of this book and the time it took me to complete it was the glue that held the project together. You have always been a strength and support for me in all that I do and I am so thankful you are mine.

My children, Canyon and Maverick, who were patient during this process as Mommy was constantly "in her cave working." All that I do is for both of you and Daddy. I love you with every inch of my soul.

My mom. My love for you was the inspiration for this book, but you have been my inspiration since I was a little girl. Your strength and beauty shine like a diamond each day and I am honored to be your daughter. Clearly, God has big plans for you and I can't wait to see what comes next.

My publisher, 5 Fold Media. Thank you, Andy and Cathy Sanders, for seeing something in this story that needed to be told. Your professionalism and knowledge have been instrumental for me and working together has been an absolute blessing. Thank you for answering my endless questions. Your heart and passion shines in all that you do.

My editors and graphic designers, for taking this book and helping to make it the best it could be. Thank you for your suggestions and investment in our story.

Family and friends who supported me over the last year, encouraging me to keep going when it got tough and sticking with me through it all. Thank you to all those who read my initial manuscript and gave me honest feedback on it. To those who consistently helped me spread the word about the book—your efforts have not gone unnoticed.

Sheila Karsevar, my dearest friend who was with me from the start, reading each chapter as it was written so I could see if this book was really possible. Your positive attitude and words of wisdom were indispensable as I began this journey into uncharted waters. God truly blessed me when He brought you into my life.

My mom's prayer warriors, who formed an army to reach God's ears in her time of deepest need. Our family will be forever grateful for those who cried out for her healing.

You, the reader, for coming with us on this journey. It was not an easy road, but it was worth every step.

Contents

FOREWORD

Does God still do miracles? Does God hear our prayers and the cry of our hearts? This is a story of how God chose to work through the cries of a few, plus an army of prayer warriors. It is a story where it seems impossible to believe that anything good could come out of the trauma.

But yes! He does hear our cries! He does answer our prayers! As this story unfolds, God will miraculously answer the prayers with a response that has no other explanation than—God!

Tricia Pawling-King shares her personal journey, interwoven with her mom's miraculous story, in such a format that you feel you are watching a movie with different scenes happening in different locations. All of these details and all of these experiences play out to an incredible ending where Romans 8:28 becomes a reality. *"And we know that God causes everything to work together for the good of those who love God and are called according to his purpose for them"* (NLT).

I was one of those many prayer warriors who were on the sidelines. We followed the story as the family's circumstances became more complex. So our prayer line was kept open as we continued to receive updates.

Having been a pastor in the same area for thirty-six years, I have known the family for many years. The reputation of Tricia's mom as an outstanding musician and director was certainly known throughout our area. Connie's standard of excellence had gained her a reputation and "name" that ultimately brought many concerned voices in prayer at this critical time.

As Tricia points out, her many moves have made it challenging to be connected to a home church, so I am pleased to have been that pastor where Tricia and Charles felt most "at home." It is my pleasure to recommend this book as a source of encouragement to all, that God hears our prayers and chooses to work in ways that go beyond our understanding. He may choose to work through doctors. He may choose to work through nutrition. He may choose to work through a miraculous intervention. Or, He may choose to use all of these to accomplish His will in our lives.

I pray that God will use this writing as a source of encouragement to you as the reader, that He will strengthen your faith and possibly point you in a new direction as you walk on your pathway! No matter what your journey holds, hold fast to the words of Jesus in Matthew 19:26: *"Humanly speaking, it is impossible. But with God everything is possible"* (NLT).

—Rev. Arlie E. Davis
Lead Pastor, Christ Wesleyan Church, Milton, Pennsylvania

INTRODUCTION

On June 28th, 2016 my mom died. For several weeks I thought it was from cardiac arrest, but when I later saw the official papers from the hospital, her reason for admittance was listed as "sudden cardiac death." Statistics show that people who experience a sudden cardiac death outside of the hospital setting have a 7 percent chance of survival. Unfortunately, most people die within moments of their heart stopping. My mom should have been just another statistic. But what happened that June day was so incredible it can only be described as miraculous.

Because she had no memory of the event, I promised my mom I would make her a journal and write down my memories of all the amazing details from that day. Two months later, I had not yet made good on my promise. But one night in late September 2016, as I attempted to go to sleep, God showed me He had His own plans. I have never felt as if God had spoken to me so clearly and directly before. He told me the journal was not enough; I needed to tell the *whole* story and should write a book to share it with others. Not just recount the details of that day but tell of miracles, both great and small, He sprinkled throughout the lives of both my mom and me in the years prior and the months to follow.

As I lay in bed that September night, my mind would not rest as I was flooded with memories. Part of me realized I should be writing them down, but another part knew they would be there in the morning, so finally, at 3 am, I fell asleep. I began writing the next day, and God breathed it all into me. Although I have never written a book, it was almost effortless. I never had a plan or an outline. I just wrote what came to me through Him.

To tell the whole story, I must go back many years to show you where it all began and the path God would lay out before us. There were difficult times along the way and things we didn't understand. But I will show you how our lives eventually melded together in God's perfect timing, not only for this day but in the days to follow. His glory would be magnified in a way that would be both awe-inspiring and lifesaving.

Come with us on this journey and find hope in the storm.

Find life, when death is surrounding you.

Find peace, when all else seems to fail.

Find light, when darkness threatens.

Ultimately, find God, when you're lost and wandering.

"For I know the plans I have for you," says the Lord. "They are plans for good and not disaster, to give you a future and a hope" (Jeremiah 29:11).

CHAPTER 1

THE TEXT

MONDAY, JUNE 27th 2016, THE POCONOS, PA

Text message to my mom at 11:39 p.m.

> "Just got off the phone with Justin...too tired
> to talk now but will call tomorrow...I think he is
> better, information is key."

W hy is that text significant? Because earlier in the day my mom was diagnosed with some of the worst news anyone can hear. Breast cancer. She had a biopsy the week prior, and we knew this diagnosis was possible. After it was confirmed, we calmly spent the day discussing her plans to move forward—how she was going to fight this cancer naturally, with no medical intervention. You see, two years prior I was introduced to life-changing nutritional products by a stranger. Since that day, I learned of hundreds of stories of people being healed from cancer because of them. So, Mom and I promised each other that if either of us ever got diagnosed with cancer, we would not go through radiation or chemo but would use these products. (I'll tell you more about that later.) We didn't think it would happen to either one of us, but now it was time for my mom to put her money where her mouth was. She had already seen some amazing results with other health issues from these products, but now she was going to put her trust in them on a much larger scale.

My mom and I have always talked nearly every day, so of course I was the first person she called to relay the news. But it wasn't until later that evening that my younger brother Justin, who was working all day, found out about the diagnosis for the first time. She told him of her plans to go natural. As soon as they hung up, Mom called me back, overwrought.

"Please call and talk to him," she pleaded breathlessly. "He is very upset and needs to know more about what I am doing. He seems scared."

Why was she asking me to call him? Because I was the one who knew the most about the products, who suggested the plan, researched it, and shared it with her.

"I will Mom, no problem; it will be fine," I assured her. "He needs more facts, and I just need to give him the assurance he is looking for."

"I will call you back later when we're done," were the last words I spoke to her that night.

I did just what my mom asked, and my brother and I talked for a very long time. When we were done, I felt I had done all I could to make him feel better. I answered the questions he had and pointed him in the right direction to see the research that had been done on the products. He is a very analytical guy, so I gave him a website to look up the published studies. All in all, I thought it was a very good call. However, by the time we were finished, it was after 11:30 p.m., and I had to get up early the next day with my children. So, I sent out the text.

"Just got off the phone with Justin…too tired to talk now but will call tomorrow…I think he is better…information is key."

I plugged in my phone to charge it, crawled into bed, and pulled the covers over me to settle in. I thought about the day, and although it would seem this would have been one of the worst days of my life, it wasn't. I was relaxed—certainly not happy about the way the day unfolded, but I was encouraged by the plan. I was confident things were, in time, going to be just fine. Little did I know the worst day of my life would begin just five hours and forty minutes later.

***

Getting news my mom had cancer was heartbreaking, but I put my trust in God's assurance that He would be with her through it all. I was not the least bit prepared, however, for what was to come.

> *This is my command—be strong and courageous! Do not be afraid or discouraged. For the Lord your God is with you wherever you go (Joshua 1:9).*

CHAPTER 2

THE CALL

TUESDAY, JUNE 28th 2016, THE POCONOS, PA

I am jolted awake from deep sleep by my vibrating cell phone. Without my contacts in, I can see very little, but a glow to my right catches my eye. I snatch my phone and see my mom's picture. At 6:19 a.m., I know such an early call cannot mean good news. As I mentioned, Mom and I speak almost daily by phone. But one thing we do not do is call each other early in the morning.

"Hello?"

"Tricia, it's Pat. I'm here with David."

Pat is her mother-in-law, and as she takes a breath before explaining the reason for her call, my fears are confirmed. This is *not* good. Not just because Pat is using my mom's phone at 6:19 a.m., but because in the moments between her taking that breath, I hear my mom's husband, Dave, in the background. And it is not just that I hear him, but I can immediately feel the agony in his tone. He is making a noise that I can only explain as guttural. It almost sounds inhuman, like a wild animal, and I will never, ever forget hearing it. I have never seen nor heard Dave cry in the nineteen years of marriage to my mom, so this emotion catches me off guard, and I brace for the raw anguish I know is next. I also feel terrible for Pat that she has to deliver it, because I sense whatever words she is about to speak will be seared into my brain for eternity. She was calling to give me news about the woman I hold closest to my heart, the woman I would do anything and everything for, the woman who has been an inspiration my entire life. And just a month earlier, my husband had fulfilled a thirteen-year-old promise to move us to my home state so we could be near her.

"Your mom went down," Pat calmly explains.

I will always be grateful to Pat, because during absolute chaos she is a rock. Slowly, carefully, she explains what she knows, but in a way that is just what I need so as not to lose my mind.

"What do you mean, down?" I beg.

Pat continues, her voice steady. "David said he was downstairs getting ready for work when he heard your mom scream. He called up to her to make sure she was all right, but she didn't answer. He ran upstairs to find her on the floor in the kitchen. She hit her head and there was blood on the floor. The ambulance just left with her, and her breathing was very shallow."

Pat had been an EMT, so shallow is a phrase that comes naturally to her. But to me, it means my mom is probably about to die. And with the sounds I continue to hear from Dave in the background, I am sure I am about to make a two-hour drive to find her gone. There will be no chance to say good-bye, no "I love you"—just here one day and gone the next. A life snuffed out in an instant like so many stories of loved ones lost in other families. But this is not someone else's story. This is my life and my family. Fear rushes through my body in a palpable wave and I begin shaking.

"I'm getting in the car," I tell her and hang up.

***

It was a good thing I didn't know the full details of that morning before my drive over because it would have made that trip even more impossible than I already felt it was going to be. To drive two hours thinking I would never talk to my mom again, and feeling anguished that the last thing I did was send her a text instead of calling her like I promised.

I learned later that the scream David heard happened around 5:40 a.m. Why then was the ambulance just leaving at 6:19 a.m. if her breathing was so shallow? They should have rushed her to the hospital as soon as possible! The reason was Mom had been dead for thirty-five minutes; that's how long the paramedics worked to bring her back. The hospital would later list her reason for admittance as sudden cardiac death—not a heart attack, not cardiac arrest, but *cardiac death*. After fifteen minutes of CPR, the paramedics asked Dave if he wanted them to stop working on her. He told them to keep going. During the thirty-five minute span, the responders used a defibrillator six times attempting to bring her back. They shocked her so many times, in fact, that she would later have a one-inch wide burn down her chest. Doctors would tell us it was the worst they had ever seen. The paramedics finally felt they had to chance moving her and decided to head for the hospital.

"Her breathing is very shallow," the words replayed over and over in my head. *This* had become the very worst day of my life.

***

I am thankful that at the lowest of my days, I had somewhere to turn and someone to rely on. God promises to help the helpless, and that's just what I was. Without Him, I would have completely fallen apart.

> *For I hold you by your right hand—I, the Lord your God. And I say to you, "Don't be afraid. I am here to help you" (Isaiah 41:13).*

CHAPTER 3

THE FACE

JANUARY 2003, MILTON, PA

I still remember—like it was yesterday—the look on my mom's face as we pulled away from the driveway of my childhood home in Pennsylvania. It was January of 2003, and my husband Charles and I decided to move from my hometown, where I lived basically my entire life, to Montana, a state on the other side of the country, twenty-four hours' drive from the family I cherished. Although I didn't realize it at the time, this move was part of the journey God set in motion long before I would ever know where it was headed or where it would end. It was an inevitable path leading to the days and years preceding that fateful day in June of 2016. To understand *why* we moved, it is necessary to look in the past.

APRIL 1998, OLEAN, NY

I was a senior at St. Bonaventure University and just finished my last college basketball game. Basketball had been a huge part of my life for the last ten years, filling my summers with pick-up games, conditioning, weight-lifting, and practice, practice, practice. But now it was over, or so I thought. As I turned my focus to my final exams, I received the most amazing news from my head coach. A newly-formed professional woman's basketball league was going to have tryouts for undrafted players. The league was in its second year after being created by the men's professional association. It's what I always wanted to do with my life, but there was no opportunity.

CANCER ON MONDAY, DEAD ON TUESDAY, HOME BY THE WEEKEND

The first ever open tryouts for the WNBA, as it came to be called, were in May. I was headed to Washington, D.C., the closest location, to try out for the Mystics, along with 360 other girls. We were all vying for one spot. Here I was, with a .002 percent chance of making my dream come true.

As day one of the tryout ended, they announced the thirty girls who would move on, and I made it! My chances had improved to .033 percent. Progress! I gave my heart and soul that next day, diving for every loose ball, pushing past the pain as my lungs burned from the effort, but as it turned out, leaving it all on the court wasn't good enough. I made another cut down to twenty, but that's where the dream ended.

That would appear to be the place to pack it in, right? It just wouldn't seem logical to continue. The chances were slim—the odds poor. But quitting was never my style, and not the type of attitude I learned from my mother. Mom was a music teacher my entire life, one the best in all Pennsylvania—at least, in my opinion and in the opinions of many others. She worked hard, she was creative, and when she did something it was with the best effort possible. She worked many hours, first during her school day and then at night with extracurricular activities, rehearsals for special musical groups, and school productions. Every year in May, she put on a school musical, and I would go all three nights to see it. I loved everything about those performances. I would sit in the audience and watch her conduct the orchestra, and I would beam with pride because the auditorium was always jam-packed with people curious to see what she came up with that year. She would not quit when rehearsals went poorly or resign herself to the thought that a particular year's musical might not be as good as productions from previous years. No, she had drive and ambition, and she inspired the kids to be the best they could. And maybe, without her knowing it, she did the same for me. She told me many times through the years that she felt guilty about all the nights she was gone, but little did she know I was still watching her, learning all the while. You don't always have to be present with your children to leave an impression. So, I was *not* giving up on my dream.

For the next year, all I did was train, condition, play, and practice, day in and day out. It was always the identical routine, but for me it was fun because this was what I loved, just as my mom loved music. Passion trumps monotony every time. I also did volunteer work with whatever spare time I had. My cousin Andy was involved with a Christian youth group, and I started helping, hanging out with the kids and teaching them about God's love. It was amazing and the first time I really remember being fully engaged in worship music. I loved the time alone with God and began to really feel connected to Him. I became a Christian at twelve, but as many stories go, for years I sort of put Him on the back burner while I did my own thing. But as I reached out to the youth group, I realized I received as much as the kids did. It was a good break from the rigorous training I was involved in each day and a chance to really see what was important in life beyond the court. I was beginning to be aware of God's hand on my life.

During that stretch, I met a new friend named Matt. In May of that year, he told me he was headed out West to work at a dude ranch for the summer in Colorado. What? Those things really existed? I had only heard about them in movies, but as he described it, it sounded amazing. He encouraged me to come with him.

"What in the world would I do there?" I asked.

He told me they had a children's program, and counselor jobs were available. I thought that would be a fun and unforgettable experience.

"You need to decide soon, though," he said, "as the spots fill up fast."

But after only a moment's consideration, I told him I couldn't do it. I refused to have a Plan B. I was making the WNBA, and that was all there was to it. The next tryout would be in Miami, and I felt confident from the work I put in. I also thought God had given me a unique opportunity that could not be denied. A good friend of mine from college, Amanda, began her career in public relations after college. Her hard work paid off, and she became head of PR for the WNBA team the Miami Sol. The team was holding open tryouts just as the Washington team had, but because of my connection to Amanda she got me past opening day. I didn't have to be one of the hundreds of people clawing to try to move on and live another day. I was already there with her help.

Now, to this day, I can't think of one good memory from that tryout. I must have done something right, but if I did I can't recall what it was. What I can recall is that despite how much I had lifted, I still got pushed around. No matter how many times I had practiced my moves, they didn't work. No matter how many times I thought I was open, I didn't get the ball. There was no reward for effort or perseverance. It was over, again. Two hours later, I was cut.

So, now what? Remember that "no Plan B" thing? No Plan B is no big deal if Plan A works out. At this point, I was reminded of a saying I am sure most of us have heard at least once in our lives:

"If you want to make God laugh, go ahead and tell Him about your plans."

Yes, my plans. Here was a good lesson: sometimes you can work as hard as possible, do everything you think you need to do to reach your goals, and yet the door is shut. In which case, you hope you feel God's nudge enough to open the window. After I was cut, I hung out with Amanda and enjoyed the time I had with her in Miami. I don't remember specifically praying that night for God to show me what to do next because the plan I was hoping for had only been over for twelve hours. But by the next day, I already felt a prompting. Without even thinking fully about what I was doing, I made a call to Matt. After that call, my life would never be the same, and I found myself on a path that could only have been predetermined by God.

The Lord directs our steps, so why try to understand everything along the way? (Proverbs 20:24)

CHAPTER 4

THE DRIVE

TUESDAY, JUNE 28th 2016, THE POCONOS, PA

I got the call from Pat at 6:19 a.m., and by 6:24 a.m. I was already dialing my younger brother Justin, who lives only minutes from Mom.

As I mentioned earlier, the desperate situation began to seize me with fear, and I was starting to become too overwrought with emotion to think clearly. Thankfully, my husband was immediately by my side and guided me down the stairs and into the garage so I wouldn't wake the kids. My breathing began to quicken, and although I have never hyperventilated there was a good chance I was about to.

"You have got to calm down," my husband said. "I can't let you drive over there like this. Think about our children if something happens to you."

Before he could say more, I answered, "I need to call my brother!"

As Justin's phone rang, I had only moments to think about what I would say to him. What words would come out my mouth that would be seared into his memory forever? I didn't have enough time to plan as I heard "*Hello.*"

"Hey. I need you to sit down," I told him.

There was nothing beautiful or elegant about it. But I knew it would get his attention without blurting out "I think Mom is going to die" and giving *him* a heart attack. I had never started a conversation by telling him to sit down. And that wasn't from a lack of difficult situations we had discussed in the past.

Here is something to know about my younger brother Justin. When there is a storm, he is your man. He is like the eye of a hurricane. The eye is so calm because the powerful surface winds that converge toward the center never reach it. That is a beautiful description of how I feel about him. It's not that he isn't distraught deep inside when there is a crisis. It's just that he does not allow the strong winds of the crisis to reach him. It's so nice to have him to rely on when I need him, and I've needed him on many occasions. I'll tell you about one of them.

***

When my oldest boy, Canyon, was three, we lived in Maine, and my husband and I decided to try for just one more child so Canyon would have a partner in this world. We had a very difficult time getting pregnant with Canyon (fifteen months to be exact), but he was born healthy. So, we thought it may take some time again, but that was okay because we weren't in a huge rush. We did our best to accept God's timing and trust in it. We were pleasantly surprised when it only took a few months for me to become pregnant again. But less than seven weeks after I conceived, we lost the baby.

Miscarriage. It's not something people talk about much, and I never even considered this would happen to us. It was devastating and impossible for us to describe our pain and anguish to other people.

Fast forward three years, with one more miscarriage in between, and we were pregnant for the third time (not counting Canyon). We were again elated, but much more cautious because we had learned that once you have two miscarriages, you are more likely to have another one. My miscarriages were also unexplained, so there was nothing for us to do but wait.

At this time we were living in Arizona, and we stopped telling people when we got pregnant. However, Canyon and I were about to travel cross country back home to Pennsylvania for a visit. Before we headed to the airport, we had breakfast with one of my good friends and her two children. I felt a small tug inside: "Just tell her." As we were leaving, I gave her a hug and whispered in her ear, "I'm pregnant!"

It was exhilarating sharing the news. Pregnancies are supposed to be times of rejoicing and celebration, yet we were no longer able to do that because of our history. So, being able to rejoice with my friend in that moment felt amazing. She was overjoyed for us, and I left the restaurant with a smile as we waved good bye.

Less than a half an hour later, as we drove the ninety minutes to the airport, I felt it. It is not a feeling I would wish on anyone. But from the experience of my other miscarriages and recognizing that specific sensation of pain, so different from any other discomfort I had previously encountered, I knew what was happening.

"Please God," I pleaded. "No, no, no, not again, not now!"

I did everything I could to wish it away. What was I going to do? I was about to make a 15-hour trip across the country with a 5-year-old while having a miscarriage. Impossible! Of course, I pulled over and called my husband first.

"Do you just want to turn around?" he asked.

I knew this was breaking his heart again, but he was always so strong for me, putting my feelings first and suffering his own pain in silence.

"It won't change anything. I'm just going to go," I replied despondently and got back in the car.

Canyon and I made it to the airport and waited for our flight. I was doing my best to stay strong for him and handle the situation, but I started to wonder how I was going to endure this. No one in my family even knew I was pregnant, and I wasn't going to be able to hide this once I got home—especially from my mom. She can tell when I am upset just by the way I say "Hello" on the phone. I just couldn't deal with telling her I lost another baby and see the devastation in her eyes, realizing the pain she felt for me and knowing there was a third baby she would never get to hold.

Then I thought—Justin! I had to call Justin. I needed strength I knew I didn't have at that moment, and I knew he could give it to me. I called and told him what was happening and within minutes he had a plan.

"You just worry about you and Canyon and get yourself home," he encouraged me. "I will take care of everything else."

Eye of the hurricane—just the calm comfort I needed. He would call every family member and tell them the news. It would take a load off my shoulders that threatened to break them.

***

TUESDAY, JUNE 28th 2016, THE POCONOS, PA

"I need you to sit down, Justin."

"I just got a call from Pat," I continued. "Mom is not good. They say she screamed and collapsed, hit her head, and is barely breathing."

I felt the need to be blunt. Was it a good choice? I don't know, but if one of us was going to have a chance to see her alive one last time, it was going to be him. I wanted to make sure he knew to get to the hospital immediately.

I don't remember anything else we said to each other. He probably does, just the way I remember every word Pat said to me, but I hoped I did a good enough job of telling him the news without scarring him for life.

"I'm on my way," he said.

Of course he was, and just knowing that made me feel better. One of Mom's children would see her again and have a memory of what might possibly be her last minutes.

I did what was essential to get out the door quickly. I put my contacts in, ran a comb through my hair, and brushed my teeth. Fortunately, I remembered to grab my phone charger on the way downstairs, as the endless use of it in the hours to come would run my battery down before noon. As I headed for the door I grabbed one more thing, which was as essential for my health as my contacts were for clear vision. Remember those nutritional supplements I mentioned? I grabbed mine because I knew this was going to be a long day, and the last thing I needed was to get sick from the stress of it all. Those supplements would prove to be part of God's master plan as the story unfolded and would give glory to His perfect design.

It was twenty-one minutes from the time I got the call to the time I got in the car. I needed a few minutes just to gather myself as my husband would not let me leave until I proved I could drive safely. I was teetering on the brink of breaking down, but after a few deep breaths coupled with the strong and loving arms of Charles's embrace, I was eventually able to stop my body from shaking and demonstrate the capability of getting behind the wheel. Two hours—how was I going to make that? And so the phone calls began. I was on the phone the entire drive. I called family members; I called friends; I called everyone I could think of to pray for my mom. Looking back, I feel worse for those who didn't answer the phone because I know my messages were blubbering run-ons of incoherent thoughts and emotions. But, I just couldn't help it. Once the tears started, there was no stopping them. I did the best I could to talk through them, but I am sure it was difficult to listen to. I did slightly better with those I actually talked to. I guess hearing another person's voice was helpful and kept me from falling apart completely. Prayers, prayers, prayers. I knew that was what we needed—a miracle from God. I continued down my contacts list, message after message. I was trying to find ways to put my mom on church prayer chains. I wanted any avenue that could reach more people and fast!

About thirty minutes into my drive, Justin called.

"I'm at the hospital. They think Mom had a heart attack, and they are taking her to the cath lab to do a heart catheterization to see if she has any blockages. The only problem is the procedure is risky, and even if she does have a blockage they are not sure she is stable enough to make it through the procedure to fix it."

I couldn't decide if this was a glimmer of good news or not. Yes, it was my first confirmation that she was still alive, but trying to find out what was wrong may possibly kill her? I couldn't wrap my head around it, but Justin delivered the news as well as he could, giving me the facts and the possible outcomes. At the moment there was nothing I could do but drive and make more calls.

When I was within an hour of the hospital, Justin called back with another update.

He relayed the latest news, "Mom made it through the catheterization, although they say she bottomed out once." (This was not a phrase I was familiar with, but I learned later that it meant her body tried to die, again, and the doctors put in a special instrument to keep her blood pressure from hitting such a dangerously low and life-threatening level.) "The good news is she has no blockages, so it wasn't a heart attack, but that's all the info they are giving me so far."

This was fantastic news, and my spirit was lifted. The last part of the drive wouldn't be nearly as difficult, and I felt a little more encouraged as I pulled into the hospital parking lot. The hardest part was over, right?

Not even close.

***

I was about to learn a hard lesson about detours. Sometimes when we feel everything will work out just fine, life makes a hard turn and shocks us to the core. Detours exercise our faith and test our hope. It is during those times we must hold tightly to God's promises to endure the pain and carry on. I needed to grab hold with all the strength I had and not let go.

> *Have mercy on me, O God, have mercy! I look to you for protection. I will hide beneath the shadow of your wings until the danger passes by (Psalms 57:1).*

CHAPTER 5

THE CHOICE

MAY 2000, MIAMI, FL

After talking to Matt, my next call was to the beautiful ranch in Colorado situated halfway up a mountain between a town called Lyons and Estes Park. The manager there informed me the season was in full swing and all the children's counselor jobs were taken. I waited too long. But, she informed me, there was a job opening in the housekeeping department.

No, thank you. I didn't even like cleaning up after myself, let alone cleaning up after someone else. In high school and college, I had practices to get to and friends to meet up with and not a minute to waste on cleaning. And now, I was being offered a job doing it eight hours a day. The horror! But again, before I could give her a list of all the reasons I couldn't do it, there was that nudge that had me saying yes before I truly understood what I was getting myself into. Not only was I accepting a less than appealing job, I was about to make a choice to move cross country, even though the farthest I had ever been from my family was in college when I lived three hours away. And yet, I felt great about the decision and headed back home to tell my mom.

I told her I would only be gone three months. I explained that I wanted to get the most out of the experience and then come back. I booked my flight with the return trip in place for August. I left for Colorado in May. By the time I arrived at the ranch that night, it was already dark, and I was nervous. But when I stepped into the sunshine the next morning, any jitters immediately disappeared. I was awestruck by what I saw. I was in the Rocky Mountains, and it was breathtaking. I thanked God for leading me out of my comfort zone and to this phenomenal place. It only took until lunchtime my first day, however, for me to realize I did not enjoy my new job. But as the days passed, I found that I looked forward to the end of my working hours, when I could sit by the stream and read my Bible or just connect with God through the beauty of this place. It washed away the unpleasantries of cleaning all day long. I loved what this place was starting to mean to me beyond my job.

A ranch like this has its own unique set up. You are miles from anywhere, and most of us didn't have a car, so we learned to bond with each other quickly. We started hanging out together in a big group. Even though we were young adults, our small community began to take on the feeling of high school. By the first week everyone started little cliques and decided who they were attracted to (there were only so many choices, and with no other people around for forty-five miles you had to move swiftly). Couples began to form, which was fine by me; a relationship was the absolute last thing on my mind.

About a month after I first arrived, I heard rumors of a "new guy." Anyone new was big news. And not only was there a new guy, he was a six-foot-four handsome cowboy from Texas named Charles. I would hear the whispers about him from the girls that I worked with, but I paid no attention. I had no time for romance.

Frankly, it was a bit of a meat market at the ranch. When fresh "product" arrived, especially one that looked good, there was a line to get to it. I thought the whole thing was comical. Charles started hanging out with our group, and I did notice he was quite handsome and fun. I wasn't looking for a relationship, so of course that's just what happened.

It wasn't until a few weeks after his arrival that I noticed when everyone else left my apartment after playing games or cards, this new guy stuck around. I have never been that observant a person, so it took me a few days to catch on.

"Did you really think I liked to play cards *that* much?" Charles would later ask me.

I hadn't really thought about it. Paying attention to those kinds of details was not one of my strengths. We began to talk late into the nights and sit together at meals, and before I knew it I was just as mesmerized by him as the other girls had been from the start. He busted his way through the wall I thought I had erected.

After only a few weeks of spending time together, Charles told me, "I am tearing up your plane ticket to go home."

I thought that was sweet, but I had my plans in place to go back to Pennsylvania, and although I was having fun I had no intention of staying. I was about to discover that God has plans we can't see, and He orchestrates things that seem impossible. Ten weeks later, we were engaged. Charles actually bought my ring after knowing me only five weeks. We went to a movie one night at the local mall, and before the show started, "just for fun" we looked at rings. He kept asking me what kind I liked. I really had no idea, because marriage was not even on my radar, but I gave my opinion and thought nothing else of it. During the previews of our movie, Charles excused himself to go to the bathroom. Little did I know he was sprinting back to the jeweler, and he immediately bought the ring he would use to propose to me a month later.

And what a proposal it was! The ranch had a beautiful chapel at the top of the mountain, and the view was phenomenal. Many times, we would hike to the top together to just enjoy quiet time alone. On one of the trips, as we were looking out toward the Rockies, he set the ring box next to me. After a few minutes, I finally noticed it. I was speechless. His proposal in that spot could not have been more wonderful and was the perfect punctuation mark to a whirlwind romance. Although I never thought I was ready for marriage, it was impossible to deny that this relationship was designed by God long before I made a leap-of-faith decision to travel this far from home.

Going to Colorado was not at all my plan; in fact, I had never even considered going out west at any point in my life. And yet I met a friend who simply suggested, "You should come." Charles would tell me months later he didn't remember ever applying for a job at the ranch.

He was working in Texas, training horses, when he got a call from the general manager.

"We need someone to run our barn. Things with the horses here need to be turned around," the manager told Charles.

Well, that's all Charles needed to hear, because (1) he loved horses, (2) he had previously worked in Colorado and loved it, and (3) he was a man of action—a quality that I would see throughout our lives in the years to come. He didn't even question the fact that he had never heard of the place before. He was a Christian, he trusted in the path that opened before him, and off he went.

To this day, we don't know where the manager got his number. But it really did not matter; a girl from Pennsylvania and a guy from Texas, who had both travelled many states to meet in Colorado, now planned to become one. God's hand? I know it was. Charles and I remained in Colorado another six months (proof it had to be love, because that was six more months of housekeeping for me) before deciding to move to Pennsylvania so I could be around my family again. We left a beautiful place we both loved, but nothing has ever compared to the beauty of being able to see my mom's face whenever I wanted. Charles has always supported my love of family, a quality I appreciate more than I could ever say, so the decision was made. We bought a car together, threw everything we owned in the back, and set off to drive across the country.

***

Although I had my own reasons for journeying to Colorado, God clearly was orchestrating my path in His direction. I am so grateful to have recognized His lead. The joy I found in my future husband and partner in this life would be immeasurable.

> *Your own ears will hear him. Right behind you a voice will say, "This is the way you should go," whether to the right or to the left (Isaiah 30:21).*

CHAPTER 6

THE NEWS

TUESDAY, JUNE 28th 2016, THE HOSPITAL

I parked my car and walked toward the entrance of the hospital. To my left I noticed a small group of friends and family members, and in the middle of them I saw my brother Justin, Mom's husband Dave, and a doctor. My guess was that the doctor was giving everyone another update; hopefully we would know more soon. I felt so much better about the situation; I didn't feel the need to rush over, so I just walked at a normal pace. I don't have very good vision, so it wasn't until I was about three feet away that I realized this was not going to be news I hoped to hear. Dave's face was dominated by a profound sadness. His eyes were red and his eyelids seemed to droop. Whatever the doctor was saying clearly had him heartbroken. But the look on Justin's face was worse. The hurricane force of the doctor's words had broken through his normal calm demeanor. His expression screamed one word when I looked at it—*pain*. The discussion ended just as I reached them. Justin and Dave pulled me aside to give me the news.

Justin said, "Since Mom had no blockages, the cardiologist says they have narrowed it down to one of three possibilities. One, Mom has an aortic tear in her heart, in which case the blood flow should make its own path around the tear, and she should start to get better. They don't think that's what it is because she is not getting any better. She is still very critical and on full life support. Two, they think it could be a blood clot caused by the breast biopsy she got last week. That is our best case and most treatable scenario, and they have already starting pumping her with blood thinners to help. Or three, she could have a brain bleed. In which case the blood thinners they are treating the possible blood clot with will likely kill her."

Pain. I understood the look on my brother's face as he concluded the possibilities with tears streaming down his face. I felt the emotion I observed contorting Dave's face as the doctor told him his wife had a 50/50 chance of making it, at best. *My* feeling was helplessness, and this is where I began to fall apart. I gave them both a quick hug and walked away. We are a very loving family, but we don't hug all the time, and no amount of affection was going to change the news we just received. I wanted to digest it alone. Just thirty minutes ago we had felt encouraged, but now our hopes were practically crushed. I began to wonder—does my mom even know she needs to fight? She had been unconscious for hours at this point, on continuous life support. Was she in an abyss of nothingness? I thought it all so unfair. She was the toughest woman I knew. She would attack this problem head on if she knew she needed to, but would she even get the chance?

At this point, I knew even without talking about it that Justin and I would both agree there was no reason to call my older brother Ryan just yet. He lived in Las Vegas and a call this early in the morning would scare him more than was necessary because we didn't have a clear vision of what was happening. It was a no-brainer to wait.

My first action was to call Charles. I attempted to keep it together as I relayed the terrible news to him and let him know I thought it was time to tell Canyon.

"You need to let him know how serious this is, and pray with him," I said.

Canyon was only nine at the time, but he had always been wise beyond his years, keenly observant of what was happening around him. I knew we couldn't keep this from him. I also didn't think it was fair to act as though Mom was going to be just fine. As I hung up, with the thought of my children possibly about to lose their grandmother (although we called her J-MA, as *grandmother* was never a name she thought fit her, so she made up her own title), all semblance of keeping it together began to deteriorate, and quickly.

Five minutes later, my phone rang. I didn't plan on answering any calls at that point because I was such a mess, but I saw it was one of my very best friends, Sheila, who I left a message for earlier. After my mom, Sheila was the person I talked to most from week to week—not only because we worked together but because she had become very important to me. Two years earlier, she was a total stranger, but now she was an integral part of my everyday life.

Sheila apologized immediately for not answering my call that morning, but it had been 6:45 am and she had her own child to take care of, so there was no reason to be sorry. I blubbered my way through the current details of my mom's condition.

Here's what you need to know about Sheila. She is one of the strongest women of faith I know, always looking for God's hand in every situation. Every time I have ever come to her with a problem, she says, "I am trying to figure out how God is going to work this out for His glory."

I rambled on about how wrong this all was. How after thirteen years of traveling we had *just* moved back to the area, and not with one child but two. How I had a miracle baby eighteen months prior, which we never thought would be possible, and now this.

"We just got here, Sheila!" I wailed. "It isn't supposed to be this way."

It's phenomenal how steady Sheila is in difficult situations. The way she listens and empathizes and then advises like her words are a direct hand of God, reaching your ears and settling you down. But at this point, I think I threw her a curve that she was not expecting to come out of my mouth, nor was I planning to say it.

"I will not survive this if she dies, Sheila. I am just telling you I won't," I confessed.

I still feel bad to this day that I blurted my raw emotions out to her, because I could feel her heart breaking for me through the phone.

"Oh Tricia," she said with a very heavy sigh.

And then she did it. I don't know how (well actually I do; remember that direct hand of God thing I talked about?), but she took a moment to compose herself and then spoke.

The Bible states, and I firmly believe, that God gives each one of us different spiritual gifts. I don't know exactly what category Sheila's falls under, but it is something special to be on the receiving end of. I can't remember what she said verbatim, but I know it was something about how *strong* my mom was and how God was going to use her story for His glory. She emphasized that *He* was in control, and she *would* survive and so would I. Her actual words were more beautifully woven into sentences and phrases that brought me back to life and revived my resolve to be strong.

I now felt the strength to stand tall and *know* God was in control, as He has always been; I just couldn't see it. But that's why they call it faith, isn't it? And by the way, the nutritional supplements I've mentioned a few times, that would continue to be a crucial part of Mom's story? The "stranger" who introduced them to me was Sheila.

I picked myself off the ground, where I had been crumpled in a heap for the last few minutes, wiped my tears, and walked back to the family. There was nothing to do now but wait. The doctor had outlined a few possibilities moving forward. If—and this seemed to be a big if—Mom improved enough to be transferred and it was a clot, she would be moved to a medical center about ninety minutes south of us immediately. If it was a brain bleed, she would be moved to a hospital about thirty minutes to our east. They would let us know either way. We gathered inside the hospital. More people showed up as the news began to travel. My mom is a very beloved lady in our area, and for good reason.

Here's what you need to know about my mom. She is absolutely beautiful, both inside and out. But her beauty goes so deep that it is difficult to even express; words do not do her justice. It's like an aura she exudes that just draws you into her. I have always been so grateful that I got to soak up most of it being her daughter. Yes, friends could enjoy her, strangers would get a feel for it just talking with her in passing, but God gave her to me as my mother and I will be forever thankful. She brings joy even in the most unusual places sometimes, because that's just who she is. Let me give you an example.

I am not much of a shopper myself, but my mom loves it. One Black Friday Mom decided she wanted to brave the insanity of the day after Thanksgiving sales and asked me to go along. I have gone with her many, many times when I didn't need anything, even though I don't really enjoy shopping. But when I get to be with my mom I don't even care; we just have fun together. As we got to the mall and started looking around, it became clear that the other people here were not having all that much fun. They were so serious, and their agendas seemed crazy. They wanted their discounts, and they wanted them now! People bumped into and jostled each other as they looked through the sale racks, squeezing through one aisle and into the next. Mom and I would just laugh as we watched the ridiculousness of it all. We took our time and went wherever there were fewer people around, regardless of missing out on some killer deals. Mom finally found one item she wanted to buy, so we got in line along with about fifteen other people. We knew what we signed up for coming out on this day, so we happily waited and chatted to pass the time. After a few minutes, though, we were again made keenly aware that others were not having the times of their lives as we heard the complaints about wait times get louder and louder.

Now, here comes the good part. You remember me saying my mom was one the finest music teachers in all of Pennsylvania, right? She is an absolute maestro on the piano and could play any piece of music you put in front of her the first time without ever seeing it before. She explained to me it was called "sight reading." I will never forget one night in high school when I noticed her get dressed up and head for the door.

"Where are you going?" I asked.

"A friend of mine needs someone to play the piano for their musical; it's opening night. Their normal pianist got sick at the last moment," she answered.

"But I don't understand. Have you ever even seen the music before?" I asked.

"No, just going to sight read it. See you later," she said as she walked out the door like it was no big deal.

After she left, I was still standing there dumbfounded, trying to sort this out in my brain. Okay, you're gonna do what? Walk into an auditorium full of hundreds of people, look at the music for the first time, and just go with it? But that was her, talented beyond measure. And not only could she play, but she had an amazing ability to teach others how to sing, possessing a very nice voice herself. Yet the sounds I heard next coming out of her mouth disproved everything I just told you about her musicality. She broke into the loudest, most awful version of "Jingle Bells" that I believe has ever been sung to this day.

"Jingle bells, jingle bells, Jingle all the waaaaaaayyyyyyy!" she crowed.

She would later tell me she was singing in what's called "tri-tones," obviously singing poorly on purpose. To this day, I have no idea what this phrase really means because I am not nearly as musical as she is. But if anybody ever asked me, this is the definition I would give: "*Tri-tones*: a type of music sung that makes others around you want to run in the opposite direction; see *ear bleeding*." It was awful. It was painful, and it was so unbelievably funny that I had to join in. I wasn't embarrassed in any way, partly because I knew this was not her real singing voice, and I didn't have to suffer a lifetime of this type of off-key melody. So here we were, two ladies out shopping on Black Friday, standing in a huge line with people jammed to our left and right who were becoming more agitated by the second at the length of their wait. But did we let them steal our joy? No way. We were belting out a Christmas tune that would make dogs join in had there been any in the area. And all of it was inspired by my mom, the music teacher. Although I can't imagine anyone in the store would have believed me if I told them that was her profession.

This was only going to go one of two ways. We were either going to agitate people so much there was going to be a riot (we were going to end up on the news, and not in a good way), or we were going to have the effect I knew my mom was going for. As I looked around, I saw people start to smile. The more they smiled, the more off key and the louder we got.

"Everybody!" I encouraged the crowd.

And this is where the whole store began to join in.

No, they didn't. That kind of thing only happens in the movies. But it did make everyone in the line settle down and have a little bit more fun.

TUESDAY, JUNE 28th 2016, THE HOSPITAL

It had been over two hours and we hadn't heard a thing—nothing good, nothing bad, radio silence. Where was our update? What was happening? It's situations like this that you realize when God gives you nothing but time, there is a whole lot more time to pray.

And so I prayed. "Send us a miracle, dear God, touch her body with your hands. Do *not* let this be the end of her story. Let her recovery be used for Your glory." Repeat, repeat, repeat.

***

Desperation. I felt like I was drowning in it. I was at such a loss I couldn't imagine any possibility of being strong throughout this crisis. But when I hit my knees, I found courage. As I admitted my weakness, I felt God's power, raising me up and giving me resilience I never thought attainable.

> *We are pressed on every side by troubles, but we are not crushed. We are perplexed, but not driven to despair. We are hunted down, but never abandoned by God. We get knocked down, but we are not destroyed (2 Corinthians 4:8-9).*

CHAPTER 7

THE MOVE

JUNE 2002, MILTON, PA

Charles and I lived in Pennsylvania about a year and a half. Because I had a teaching degree, I could substitute teach during the week and waitress on weekends. There were no ranches to speak of in the area or any horses to train, so Charles bartended. It was a sacrifice he was making for me, and we were happy. We bought my childhood home from my mom, who moved across the river with her husband Dave. As much as we enjoyed our lives, we did not want to do these jobs forever. So as the school year wound down, I began looking for job opportunities to get a full-time teaching position in the area for the next year. As luck would have it, there was a posting for a second grade teacher at the same elementary school I attended as a child. This was amazing timing, as it is a small school and openings were not always available. The hiring principal was a man I had known my whole life. He watched me grow up, become Salutatorian of my graduating class, and get a college scholarship to play Division 1 basketball. Could it get any better? Not only would he be looking at my credentials on a resume, but he would also know the person behind the piece of paper. It was perfect. God's plan was lining up before me, just as plain as day. I am certain at this point God let out the slightest of giggles at my certainty.

I went in for my interview. I felt prepared. Granted, it was the first interview I had ever been on, but I have always felt comfortable with people and considered myself to be well spoken. I felt confident in answering questions regarding how to be a successful teacher and thought I could handle anything they threw my way. I spoke of my experience coaching basketball. Not only had I coached at the collegiate level for a year, but Charles and I led a seventh grade girls team to a 15-1 season that past spring. I gave him more reasons to hire me, as I could be an asset to the district for their sports teams. I walked out of the school feeling good; the way I saw it, there was no reason why I would not get an opportunity for a second interview. But there's where the problem was: how I saw it.

My perception and the principal's were apparently on totally different levels—so much so that I was not asked back. I replayed the interview over and over in my mind. Did I do a good job? I thought so. Well, maybe I did stumble a few times and maybe I did guess once or twice at what they wanted to hear. But all in all, I thought it was sufficient. I mean, come on, the principal knew me personally; that must count for something. Yet it was obviously not good enough. All the extra advantages I thought I had going in had not been enough to even move me to the next round let alone get me the job. I was at a loss. Looking back, I can picture God smiling up in heaven at this point, reminding me, "Not your will child, but Mine." When I realized a second interview was not coming, Charles and I talked about what the future held for us.

He said, "Well, if you can't get a teaching job, then we'll go with what I do."

That sounded like a plan. I did not fully comprehend at the time that what he did was mostly based out west. Ranches in Pennsylvania were not common in job openings that I had seen. Yet, I still believed he could find something relatively close. I never really asked in what areas he was looking. He began to send out resumes furiously.

"I've got an interview," he told me a few months later.

"Great, where is it?" I asked.

"Montana."

I'm sorry, what? Montana, as in the state closer to the Pacific Ocean than to the Atlantic? I don't think so. The other side of the country was not in my realm of possibilities.

46

"Just let me at least fly out there and see what I think," he continued.

I truly didn't think much would come of it because (1) I wasn't really considering it whole-heartedly, but I also wasn't going to deny him a chance to see the place, and (2) what were the chances really that this whole thing would work out? He had to be offered the job. It had to be the right salary. We needed proper housing and reimbursement for our move cross country. There was no way all those things were going to line up perfectly.

Wrong again.

Charles came back and showed me video of the property and gave me the job description. The place and the opportunity were one of a kind, to say the least. It was a 1,000-acre private ranch, owned by a woman from Newport Beach, California who only visited three times a year. There would be a few weeks of visitors in the summers, but winters would be very slow. We would pretty much be on our own schedule, with maintaining the property our only duty. She would provide us with a beautiful home on the property with huge glass windows boasting a view of the Rocky Mountains from the deck and a pond beyond the front yard. We could do anything we wanted to the house to make it more our own. Charles would manage the place and take care of the twenty-three horses she owned, along with other buildings on the property, including an amazing lodge and three cabins. He would take guests on horseback rides through the property when they came in the summer, and snowmobiling in the winter. Tough gig! The salary she offered was reasonable, and she would pay for our move.

Wow. This was not how I planned for this to go at all. But I had to consider it because of all the sacrifices Charles willingly made for me. He didn't push for us to follow his career but was supportive of my teaching aspirations and ready to adapt his career long term depending on where I got a job. We prayed about it, and there was no denying that this was where God was truly leading us. It was not the path I laid out with the teaching opportunity, where I got the job and then tried to give God the credit afterward. Learning not to question God's lead was a lesson I would have to embrace many times in the years to come, even when I didn't understand it.

The day arrived. Our belongings were loaded in the back and our dogs were taking up all the available space in the front of the moving truck. This left me with about a two-foot space in which to squeeze myself for what would turn into a three-day journey to Montana. All that was left to do now was wave good-bye and head out. At the last moment, I turned to take one last look at my mom, standing near the driveway. Her sadness was so heavy and suffocating that her face wore an expression that was unforgettable. Her only daughter was starting a new chapter in her married life; she was pretty sure she liked this guy, but now he was taking me two thousand miles away. But she would tell me in the months to follow that Charles promised her he would find a way to bring me back home to her eventually. No matter how long it would take, God willing he would make it happen.

> *Trust in the Lord with all your heart; do not depend on your own understanding. Seek his will in all you do, and he will show you which path to take (Proverbs 3:5-6).*

CHAPTER 8

THE WAIT

TUESDAY, JUNE 28th 2016, THE HOSPITAL

By noon a member of the hospital care staff informed our group that we could head up to the ICU waiting room to wait for word of Mom's condition. But that was all she said. This news was both good and bad for us. It had been nearly three and a half hours since we last heard from anybody. As a family, we had not been thrilled with the communication we had received throughout the morning, but we had to trust it was because they were doing everything they could to save Mom's life. So, we dealt with it. There was nothing we were going to be able to do anyway.

"Maybe this is a good sign," Dave said when we sat down again. "Maybe that means she's stable enough to be up here and in a room."

Glass half full. I liked it. But that didn't mean any of us really felt good about that being the case; especially when no doctors said anything to support that line of thinking. The thought ran through my mind, "Maybe she is already gone, and they are just not telling us." When you hear nothing, you begin to fill in the gaps with worst case scenarios; it's just human nature. It was not a thought I would ever say out loud, but I was still thinking it. I willed myself to stay positive.

I sat with my grandmother on a couch (we call her Mimi as no one in this family seems to accept *grandmother* as their title). She was eighty-seven years old and a pillar of strength. But the day's stress was getting to her. She laid her head on my shoulder, exhausted. I put my arm around her and thought about how frightening it must be—the possibility of losing your child. I have always heard people say burying your own child is something no one should ever have to endure. Mimi and Mom are both Christians, so Mimi knew where Mom was headed if she died, but there's no way that would make the current pain go away. My grandfather just died the year before, in the same hospital. He was moved to this exact ICU floor on life support in the days before he passed, just like Mom. There was nothing easy about the scenario Mimi was facing again.

Here's what you need to know about my Mimi. At eighty-seven, she continued to work, having spent over fifty years at the same job, always just as dedicated as the day she started. She worked at a peanut factory and was highly adored and addressed as "Peanut Packing Peg." Still vibrant, she worked just as hard as anyone else there. I remember I worked with her at this place for one week when I was in high school. It was all I could do. It was not easy and quite monotonous. One week was my limit. But here was my Mimi, still going to her job with joy in her spirit and a positive attitude. I believe this was where my mom learned it; these qualities start at the top.

As Mimi laid her head on my shoulder, I remembered the phone call to her that morning. It was the first I made after I spoke to Justin. And even though we were in the middle of the most trying day of my life, I let the memory of it break a small crack in the tension of my body.

***

I knew Mimi was always up early and would be awake when I called.

"Hello," she answered.

"Mimi, it's Tricia," I said.

"Who?"

"TRICIA."

"Tricia?"

50

"Yes Mimi, it's *TRICIA*," I replied and continued to increase my volume each time. This was not going to be an easy conversation to start with, and at this pace it was going to be even worse. Then it hit me.

"Mimi, do you have your *hearing aids* in?" I questioned her.

Mimi has always been in fabulous health. Yet her hearing was less than perfect, so she wore hearing aids. But they annoyed her sometimes, and she did not always use them.

"Oh no, sweetie, I haven't put them in yet," she confessed.

"Mimi, I am going to *need* you to go get them before we talk any more."

It kind of made me giggle thinking back on the absurdity of trying to deliver such critical information to someone who could not hear me.

"Okay, be right back," she said in her cheerful voice.

Oh Mimi, she didn't get offended that I asked her to put them in. She just pleasantly complied and went off in search of them. She is something else. I was about to deliver terrible news, and in the moments before she was just as chipper as could be.

But it was this brief conversation before we got serious that made me think of a TV show I used to watch called *Roseanne*. Not many shows make you laugh out loud, but this one did for me, even after seeing every episode multiple times. There was one episode that reminded me of this conversation and gave me a moment's break from reality, allowing me to smile and stop thinking about the gravity of the situation.

On the show, Roseanne's dad died. Of course, death is not a normal cause for comedy, but in this instance, it was. It wasn't real, so it felt okay to laugh. Roseanne put her sister Jackie in charge of making the phone calls to inform the family. Her first call was to their ninety-year-old grandmother they called Nana, who didn't hear very well either.

"Nana, I'm calling with some terrible news," Jackie revealed to her.

"What?" Nana responded.

"I have bad news," Jackie repeated. "Nana, Dad is *dead*."

"Whhaatt?"

"*Dead*," she yelled more clearly and deliberately. "Dad's *dead*!"

"He's *whhaatt*?" Nana began increasing her own volume.

"*Dead. Dead. Dead.* He's *deeaadd!*" Jackie screamed, holding the phone from her mouth and screeching as her face turned beet red.

"I'm sorry Jackie, *what* did you say?" Nana asked one last time, just as clueless.

"Nothing, Nana. Dad is fine, he sends his love." Jackie replied and dropped the phone to the floor. She turned to Roseanne and said, "You can't *make* me do that again!" and walked out of the room.

* * *

This scenario was a break from reality, a brief respite. I realized through this day that you had to occasionally find a way to stop thinking about the worst that could happen. It also made me smile because Mom knew how much I loved that show, and she would have been laughing right along with me had we been watching it together. I would go shopping with her even though it wasn't my thing, and she would watch shows with me that weren't really her taste just because I liked them. We were two peas in a pod that way. But now my mind quickly returned to the present as Mimi leaned on me for support. This had to work out. Mimi could not lose her husband and her daughter in such a short time span. It was unthinkable.

Moments later, we received some good news. We finally found out that doctors read the CAT scan results and could confirm that Mom did not have a brain bleed. Hallelujah!

We didn't hear this update from a doctor, however. Dave ran into someone in the hallway and pleaded for information. He wasn't even on the ICU floor when he got the update. He was in the Emergency Room, because in addition to his wife being in critical condition, his father had just been rushed to the same hospital with signs of a stroke. Could this day get any worse for Dave? Probably not, but God's perfect timing had been evident throughout the day, undeniably, and now we had two examples of it from that morning.

Earlier that morning, Mom's House: Hand of God Part 1

5:45 am

Dave was downstairs getting ready for work. He knew my mom was upstairs getting his lunch ready as she does each day. He heard her scream.

"Connie?" he called up to her.

No response. He immediately bolted up the steps. Now for me, I still think this part is amazing. Maybe it was the type of scream she let out or something specific about the way she did it that alerted him something was wrong. He's never told me. Many times I have been in a house and heard someone scream. Maybe they slammed their fingers in a door or bit their tongue or stubbed their toe? Thankfully for my mom and all of us who love her, Dave did not wait a few minutes to check on her. From the story I've heard since, even one minute would have been too late.

When Dave reached the kitchen, his worst nightmare was playing out in front of his eyes. His wife was slumped on the tiled kitchen floor next to the refrigerator with the door still open. She was turning gray and taking her very last breaths of life, gasping for air. He could see blood on the floor where she obviously hit her head when she fell. She fell on a tile floor from a standing position, so there was even more cause for concern.

If her fall had happened even fifteen minutes later, Dave would have already left for work, so Mom would have been alone, unable to call for help, and she would have died. God's perfect timing on full display.

Without a second thought, Dave began CPR. Doing lifesaving CPR on your own spouse must do something to you deep inside that you could never fully vocalize. Flashing back to the phone call I received from Pat, I thought of the sounds Dave was making once my mom was headed out the door and into the waiting ambulance. Guttural sounds that were his release of anguish in the moments that followed this tragedy. I can now understand what made him overcome with emotion to the point of making noises that would convey a pain so deep, even he probably couldn't understand it.

So how is it that Dave knows CPR and knew enough to spring into action without being in shock? Interesting story. At this point, Mom and Dave had been married nineteen years. There were things I knew about Dave and things I knew about their marriage. He loved car racing and would have loved to do it as a profession. He relished the rush of adrenaline he received from it. Dave grew up on a farm and became an excellent heavy machine operator, using equipment such as excavators and bulldozers. Before he met my mom, he channeled his love of the adrenaline rush into working as a volunteer firefighter, and he was very dedicated to it. Maybe in my mom's view a bit too dedicated for her taste, because *every* Tuesday night he would go to training and sometimes even have special trainings on the weekends. With an already busy schedule between the two of them, it was just one more commitment she wished he didn't have week in and week out.

It would also interrupt different events in their lives because he wore a pager. If it went off, he would drop everything and head to the fire station. This tended to happen in the middle of the night, and although some people can go right back to sleep, my mom couldn't. She would be up for good, which did not make her happy. I would venture to say at times it was a point of contention in their marriage. But Dave used to explain to her that people needed the volunteers in this rural area. *What if they don't have us to rely on? What if that's you someday?* I don't think she could do much arguing about it, but that didn't mean she had to like it either. Yet, when my mom later became fully aware of what he did that morning to save her life, I am sure it was one argument she was glad she didn't win. She would be amazed at how something that caused such issues in their marriage would be the exact reason she was still alive. This was a designed path for Dave's life God set in motion long before Mom even knew him. It started more than twenty years before that day and before Mom would need Dave's help so desperately.

**

I am so weak in my understanding of God. I always want to know what is happening and for what reason. Confusion comes from my own need to control. Yet as I got a glimpse of God's glorious timing on a day my mom needed perfection, I saw His hands are always on our lives—every moment, every day.

> *Jesus looked at them intently and said, "Humanly speaking, it is impossible. But not with God. Everything is possible with God" (Mark 10:27).*

CHAPTER 9

THE QUESTION

6:00 a.m., MOM'S HOUSE, PA

Somehow, along with saving his wife's life, Dave not only called 911 but also his mother, Pat. She only lived five minutes away, and he needed her for support. The paramedics arrived in an amazingly short amount of time. They came from the same fire station Dave volunteered for and were stationed less than half a mile from their house. Dave had since retired from being a firefighter and not received CPR training in over two years, and yet he remembered. He kept my mom alive until they got there. There is a new machine that does the chest compressions for the paramedics, so they have their hands free to do other assessments and treatments. The contraption is placed over you and puts the exact amount of pressure needed (which I have always heard is a lot, just this side of breaking your ribs to be successful), and it never gets tired like a human. I've been told it looks a little barbaric, but I will always be grateful it was invented in time for this day as the machine would do compressions on my mom for close to forty minutes. I guarantee for that length of time, human hands and bodies would not have done it perfectly or continued without getting tired.

Dave told me the standard amount of time for bringing someone back to life is fifteen minutes. After that time elapsed, the paramedics asked Dave a question. Do you want us to continue? Their first fifteen minutes combined with the ten he did meant she had been down for twenty-five minutes already. Would she even be herself if they brought her back? Would she be brain damaged? I know my mom would never want to come back if she was not going to be a healthy person again, but there was no time for second guessing, and Dave urged them to continue.

At that point, there was nothing Dave and Pat could do but watch. Watch Mom's chest as it was being thumped continuously, while they pumped air into her lungs and stood helpless as she flat-lined, time after time. "*Clear,*" was all they heard as Mom was shocked multiple times to restart her heart. It was never a word that meant much to me. You hear it all the time on doctor shows, and sometimes you watch as it takes multiple attempts to bring someone back. I think maybe three or four times is the most I have ever seen on TV. Then people either come back to life or they call it—time of death 0615 hours, they'd say. So, knowing that my mom was shocked over and over and that Dave had to see her body so lifeless is unfathomable to me. The paramedics made the decision that she was as good as she was going to get and knew they needed to get her to the hospital. After close to forty minutes, at least she had "*shallow breathing,*" as Pat described. They knew additional help was needed if she was going to have a chance of survival. We never got many details of her exact condition when she arrived at the hospital, although we know she was clinging to life and shocked additionally in the ambulance with continuous CPR the whole way there. The trauma her body was going through seemed like too much to recover from.

7:15 a.m., Hand of God: Part 2

Dave and Pat arrived at the hospital and were anxiously waiting to hear any news of Mom's condition. During their wait, Pat decided to call her husband, Bob, Dave's father. This is the other part of the morning I find fascinating. I'm sure I would have called my husband eventually, but I may have been a bit distracted, at least for a while with all Pat just witnessed and experienced. Yet, she quickly phoned Bob. As she started to relay the details of the last hour, she noticed something "off" about the way he was talking. He seemed to be slurring his words. Pat and Bob had been married a few decades, so she was intimately in tune with him. The fact that she did not just race through the list of events on auto pilot, hurrying to get off the phone and back to Dave, but really listened to what Bob said in return may have changed his life. As soon as they hung up, she immediately called an ambulance, and it turned out her instincts were correct. She called Bob in the middle of a stroke, within a window of time so small the coordination had to be perfect. With Pat gone at the hospital with Dave, already joined by one of Dave's brothers with the other on the way, there was no one who would have found Bob as he had the stroke. And yet, because of the timing of that phone call, Bob was brought in and treated immediately. Later that day, we found out he would have no long-term effects from his stroke. Miraculous.

THE ICU

By early afternoon, we continued to wait anxiously in the ICU family room. A hospital volunteer, who just happened to be a family friend, approached me.

"Do you want to try to see her?" she asked.

"Yes, more than anything," I pleaded.

"Well, I don't see any reason why we can't try," she said.

My brother had stepped outside for a few minutes, so I went alone with her through the doors to the ICU. I was immediately struck with a sick feeling and began to have second thoughts, because not knowing anything now seemed better than seeing Mom on her death bed. As we approached the nurses' station, my friend told the woman at the desk I was Connie's daughter and would like to see her, if only for a moment.

"She's right across the hall," she answered, "but this is not a good time."

My sick feeling was confirmed. We had no news because there wasn't anything good to tell us. Doctors were packed in her room so tightly that I couldn't even get a glimpse of her. They still had no idea what was wrong with her and called all hands on deck to try to figure out her condition before she coded again. I am sure by this point her body could not possibly take much more.

"They are working hard to help her," the nurse assured me. "She is still unconscious and on life support. Try coming back a little later."

Well, if possible that information only seemed to makes things worse for me. So many hours later, she was still struggling to stay alive.

Just as we were leaving, the volunteer whispered to me, "You know I did hear someone say your mom woke up for a moment and started thrashing around a bit. They immediately had to sedate her so she didn't tear out her IVs."

Now that sounded like my mom, ready to fight whatever situation she was handed. Obviously, when she awoke she had no idea what was happening and got extremely agitated and scared. I hated knowing she was so upset, but this was our first sign that the prayers were working. She was conscious for the first time in almost six hours. God's prayer warriors were becoming an army, and He was answering their calls for help!

We walked back to the waiting room, and I told my brother the news. It was the first time I saw the tension break from his face all day. She was not out of the woods yet. The doctors still didn't even know what was wrong with her, so how could they treat her? But she was alive and fighting mad—if only for a moment—and I bowed my head to say thank you and give credit where credit was due.

**

I could picture the masses of people praying for my mom, engaging in the ultimate battle for life. A spiritual army of God's children crying out for help, lifting their prayers to the ultimate physician. The power of prayer was undeniable.

The Lord himself will fight for you. Just stay calm (Exodus 14:14).

CHAPTER 10

THE RANCH

2003, MONTANA

Charles and I loved everything about living at the ranch in Montana. Being in nature was our element. We were different from a lot of couples we knew because the more time we spent together, the better we got along. The environment was magical and perfect for us in every way. We also got to share this wonderful place with our family.

Mom and Dave made a few trips out west to see us. During one stay, Dave and I started talking about Mom's recent health issues. Remember the joy I talked about that exuded from her? Well, it was still there, but at this point in her life it was a lot less natural and took much more effort. Five years earlier, a pain crept into her neck that would become her constant, unrelenting companion every day, every hour. This became a difficult issue for my mom because she was an educator and had to teach, play the piano, and run rehearsals all throughout the school year. Not only did she have these commitments, but they all took a highly positive, energetic, and enthusiastic nature to be successful. This was not a problem for her normally, because that was who she was at heart. But add a chronic pain in her neck, which she would describe as having a bowling bowl for a head, and the suffering that came with it, and she now had a problem. Adding to her distress was the fact that doctors told her there was no solution.

She tried everything those five years to alleviate her issue—acupuncture, chiropractic, Rolfing (a form of very deep massage), and every cream, ointment, or supplement anyone suggested. She was desperate for help and tried anything possible, until there was nothing left to do. She was officially diagnosed with something called myofascial pain syndrome, which simply means she had chronic muscular pain. But having a diagnosis without an effective treatment plan is a difficult reality to absorb. After everything she tried failed, the only option the doctors gave her was to go on two different narcotics to help with the pain. She should try to enjoy life the best she could. But while encouraging her to do her best to deal with it and be happy, they also prescribed an anti-depressant. Doctors saw this type of chronic pain enough to know life was going to be extremely difficult each day, and it was never going to get better. Her pain was not going away because there was no cure for it, and it was going to be depressing knowing this was now her life. Their only advice was to handle it and take her pills daily.

The narcotics never took the pain away, they only "took the edge off." During her school day, Mom had to go to the faculty room multiple times to lay down because she could not hold her head up for eight hours straight. She is an extremely tough lady, but even the strongest of women can only handle so much.

Mom and I talked about her pain all the time because we were so connected. Although I couldn't see it, I knew it was there and tried to empathize the best I could and let her talk about her difficulties. I knew that was all I could do for her—that and to pray for a miracle every day from the time she was diagnosed. But five years passed with no signs of a miracle, so reality was that those narcotics were the only things helping her function on a normal basis at all. And she did an amazing job. I wouldn't fully know how much she was "faking it" daily until years later.

By the following year, she reluctantly had to lay down her sword. The fight was over. She could not take another day of teaching, even though it was her passion for over twenty years. She had planned on doing it for years to come. But at the age of 55, she was forced into disability retirement. This was a very tough decision for her, but she had no other choice. Sometimes life chooses for us and doesn't ask our opinion.

THANKSGIVING 2004, MONTANA

We had been in Montana almost two years and relished the experience. Although we loved where we were, living so far from family had its obvious disadvantages. I was used to being around for every holiday, and we now missed everything but Christmas. However, even with being so far away on Thanksgiving, we had reason to celebrate. After three years of marriage, Charles and I were ready to have a child. I thought it would be an easy process, as my grandmother got pregnant quickly, and my mom said all she had to do was look at my dad to get pregnant. I assumed this was some sort of genetic thing they would pass down to me. Apparently, I was wrong. It had taken fifteen months for us to get a positive pregnancy test, but now the day was here, and we were ecstatic.

We called Mom first to share the news. Two thousand miles was not enough distance to keep me from feeling the electricity of Mom's happiness reach me instantly. Her only daughter was about to have a child, and she couldn't wait. But clearly, there was still a problem. How often would she see her grandchild? My younger brother Justin and his wife already had a son she could see any time she wanted, because they lived within five miles of her. But with me living on the other side of the country, that was not going to be an option. It had to be something she considered and was saddened by, even with this joyous news. Little did she know, God already stirred this thinking in our hearts, and even though we loved Montana we were already sending out resumes. Now that we were pregnant, Charles was attempting to make good on his promise to her. We now needed to wait to see if God would make a way.

***

There were many things in our lives we wanted to work out the way we designed them in our heads. But as children of God, my husband and I committed to following where we were led. We always prayed for God's will and did our best to follow.

When the Spirit of truth comes, he will guide you into all truth. He will not speak on his own but will tell you what he has heard. He will tell you about the future (John 16:13).

CHAPTER 11

THE ASCENT

TUESDAY, JUNE 28ᵗʰ 2016, THE HOSPITAL

I t was 2:00 p.m., the ICU waiting room was full, and we received word that prayer chains were active in many of the surrounding towns. Dave's brother also posted about Mom online to help reach more people in the shortest amount of time and to encourage continual prayer. Justin and I finally took a few minutes to get a bite to eat, and it was nice to get a small break. We didn't talk all that much in the cafeteria, but just being together was comforting. Also, knowing that Mom had woken up for a moment was enough of a comfort that we could enjoy the short time away from the ICU. We still didn't know where things would go from here, but just knowing I'd have Justin with me through the good or the bad, for the duration of this day, meant more than I could explain.

Justin is almost five years younger than me, so when he started high school, I was already in college. I didn't really get to see him grow from a boy to a man. I also missed out on most of his sporting events, which was unfortunate because he was very talented in both football and basketball. He was so talented, in fact, that when I was training for the WNBA, I asked him to help me. He is 5'10" and an excellent defensive player, so I thought, if I could score on him, I should be able to score on a girl much easier. Many times, I never scored at all, but I knew the experience was paying off. Whenever I have truly needed help, and not just with sports, he has never let me down. We always enjoyed spending time together when I was on break from college. We have similar character traits that make it fun to be with each other. We both love to have a good time and make people laugh. I feel we've always had an unspoken bond between us that allows us to trust each other completely, and words aren't always necessary. Even though I missed a lot of his formative years, I was now reminded of what a strong man he became. We headed back upstairs to join everyone else, and I felt better than I had all day, especially with him by my side.

As we walked into the waiting room, we heard Dave got a chance to see my mom. This was encouraging for me. If he can see her, she must not be dying. Any glimmer of good news was something to hold on to tightly. After fifteen more minutes of waiting, Justin and I couldn't take it any longer, and we walked through the double doors to the ICU rooms. We just *had* to see her. Dave was walking out the door as we reached Mom's room, and we talked briefly. He said she wasn't awake, but we didn't care; just to be able to sit by her side and hold her warm hands at this point was enough. We flanked her on both sides and did just that.

Although I was so grateful to finally be in the same room with her after seven hours, looking at her in this condition was beyond difficult. She had a breathing tube covering most of her face, and more IVs than I could count. I could see her hair matted in the back where she hit her head, and there was still dried blood. Apparently, they didn't clean that yet, just put a gauze pad on it and moved on. Having any sort of damage from where she hit her head didn't matter if she was not alive, so they decided at the moment it was inconsequential. That was a little tough to comprehend because I worried about brain damage. But my only choice was to trust what they were saying. What was even more nerve-wracking was looking at the machines and all their numbers, especially because I didn't know what most of them meant. I recognized the blood pressure numbers, though, and those numbers kept me on edge. We all know perfect pressure is 120/80, and I am no doctor, but as I watched her pressure linger at 80/45, I was less than encouraged. Every time I watched the bottom number dip, even a point, I could feel my own blood pressure rising. I felt like any moment an alarm was going to sound, and I was going to witness another code.

Justin and I sat in silence, just caressing her hands and looking at her for quite a while until a doctor finally came in. He was a very relaxed man, and Justin and I both commented later how he always had his hands in his pockets, like things were no big deal. In a way, it was oddly comforting. He walked over to one of the machines and stared intently, without saying a word, for several minutes. I am someone who shows each emotion on my face, so I watched his every move hoping to get a read on him. I couldn't see any change of expression at all. Like I said, very laid back, but I appreciated that about him. When we thought we weren't interrupting, we finally asked for some information.

"No one had updated you?" he asked.

Uh no, not for like six hours if we're being specific. I didn't say that out loud, though, because at this point it didn't matter. She was alive, although still not breathing on her own, but alive all the same. And the updating wasn't his fault. Mom had just been transferred to his care in the ICU, and he had been trying desperately to figure out what was wrong with her.

"Well, we still don't know anything concrete," he explained. "She had an EKG earlier and we are still waiting for the results that may tell us more about the condition of her heart. All we have basically been able to do at this point is eliminate things. It wasn't a heart attack, a brain bleed, or a clot. But we still aren't any closer to what it was. We are just waiting to see if the EKG shows us something new."

"Is she stable?" I asked.

It was the only word I hoped to hear all day—stable. Not because people who are stable don't ever eventually die. It's just that I wanted her body to have a break to regain some strength in case something else went wrong. Being stable for any length of time seemed like it would help.

He answered, "Well, we can't possibly call her stable when we don't know what's wrong with her. But from the notes I've read about the condition she was in when she arrived this morning, the fact that she is alive at all at this point is phenomenal. The whole hospital is talking

67

about it. However, we won't know if she will have any brain damage until a few days have passed."

This was a scary sentence, but as terrible as it seemed, brain damage apparently was on the back burner at this point.

He continued, "The good news is that all morning she has been on full oxygen, and now when I look at her numbers, she is starting to take over breathing herself. If she continues to improve in this manner, we may be able to take her off the breathing machine tonight."

Unbelievable. He was admitting there was nothing specific they did to make her any better. They truly did not know how to help her at this point, and yet she had begun her ascent. I will always respect and honor doctors for the work that they do, but clearly there were other hands on her this day, and they did not belong to anybody wearing a white coat.

He also explained more about the moment she woke up. He said she was so agitated they had to paralyze her. The word *paralyze* in the same sentence with my mom was not a pleasant thing to hear. But he emphasized it was necessary, because they planned to put in a specific type of IV called a PICC line that would allow multiple lines of medicine to be administered simultaneously. They couldn't allow her to cause a problem, because it could be dangerous. Okay, I guess that seemed reasonable. His words were confirmed when Dave had to sign papers allowing this IV, because although 100 percent necessary, the procedure had its risks. Yet, there was no possibility of saying no, because she needed all the help she could get. The doctor explained they needed to do it quickly, because her paralytic medication would wear off soon, and they were afraid she would try to rip out the IVs. So, we left them to their work, and headed together back to the waiting room. Yes, things were looking up, but she obviously had a long way to go.

We gave the update to everyone still waiting for news. No one had left; in fact, the only change was that more people came. Dave told them of Mom's present condition and their plans to put in the new line. She had made good strides, yet brain damage was still possible, and we had no answers. He asked that they continue to pray. My mom's and Dave's pastor, who had been at the hospital since early that morning, asked us to join hands. We made a large circle and bowed our heads. He released a strong and moving prayer and opened it up for anyone else to speak when he finished. Dave began his appeal to God to give him his wife back, healthy and strong. I don't remember much of what he said, partly because he was crying so hard it was impossible to understand. But that didn't matter; God knew his heart, and his words were as clear as a blue summer sky to Him. This was His child, and He knew what Dave would say this day even before Dave did. Dave bared his soul in those moments. He allowed himself a release from every pressure this day had laid upon him and thanked God for what He was doing in Mom's body. He also asked God continue to heal and bring glory to His name through her recovery. As we concluded with an amen, we were hopeful and eager to hear more good news.

***

Tragedy happens and we become lost. I know our whole family felt that way. When people say life changes in an instant, they speak the truth. One moment my mom was healthy, the next she was dead. But there was glory to come through healing, praises to be given. I watched in silent awe as God laid His hands on my mom and began to raise her from the clutches of darkness.

> *But when Jesus heard about it he said, "Lazarus's sickness will not end in death. No, it happened for the glory of God so that the Son of God will receive glory from this (John 11:4).*

CHAPTER 12

THE START

MONTANA

It was January of 2005 when Charles found a new job on a small private ranch in upstate New York. We were thrilled! It was the same work he did in Montana, just on a smaller scale. We headed back across the country but weren't scheduled to start working until the end of the month, so we stopped at Mom's house to spend a few weeks. I was closing in on four months pregnant at this point, and it was nice to share that time with the family, if only for a small window. As it grew close to the time to leave for New York and start the new job, Charles sensed my hesitation to pack up.

"You don't want to go anymore, do you?" he asked.

He knew me so well because I didn't even mention anything to him. But as I said, I wear my emotions on my face, so my face was speaking to him without me needing to use any words. The more we thought about it, we weren't sure that me trying to help on a ranch while pregnant *was* the best option. With this being our first child, we also really wanted to be close to those we loved to share the joy with them. So, we stayed. Pregnant and without jobs. We gave up an excellent opportunity but believed God would provide and remain faithful.

I went back to my old waitress job so we had some instant income. Charles looked for something more career oriented. He knew he must support us fully once the baby came, and eventually he got an interview for an assistant general manager position at a resort near the Poconos. Even he was a bit surprised, because he truly did not have the experience needed. Ranches and resorts are totally different animals, but nonetheless, he had a shot.

Here's what you need to know about Charles. In the fifteen years we've been married, he's had many interviews over the phone. But, whenever he has a chance for a face to face, it's usually "game over" for the other applicants. I have never actually talked to anyone who's interviewed him, but I know he must have something so special about the way he presents himself because nine out of ten times, he is offered the job. Now, not every job has been the right fit for us, nor does he always accept them, but he has a charisma that must be mesmerizing. I know this is something special God put in him. This quality paved the way to get us to the multiple locations where God obviously had planned for us to be. I've always been so proud of the way Charles provided for our family.

After his interview for a job he was not fully qualified for, he did it again and was hired immediately. The only issue was the resort was an hour away, but we were thankful for his opportunity and tried our best to make it work. A few months after Canyon was born, however, the commute began to be a problem. We made the move to live on the resort where he worked. It was much more expensive to live there, but it would cut down on gas and his time away from us. We still lived within an hour of family, so it was no big deal. After about seven months, we realized living on this resort was just too costly for his salary. He made the decision to transfer to the resort's sales department, providing the opportunity to make more money to cover our daily needs.

It's amazing how quickly things can change. It his first year, Charles was one of the top salesmen in the entire company, providing all we needed and much more. But during the second year, things slowed down just a little for him. He was still producing very well, but business is business, and you are only as valuable as the money you make for the company. They began to cut his commissions just because they could. Fortunately, Charles has always been one to prepare for a storm, and he knew this was not going to work long term. This company showed no signs of caring about its people.

A few months later, we broke the news to my family. We were leaving, again. I felt terrible for my mom, as we had just come back. She only got two years to spend with Canyon, and now we were taking him away. Yet we cannot always control how things go, and as always, we prayed for answers. The answer took us to Maine. It was nine hours away but still a one-day trip. We packed up our house—something I would become a pro at in the years to come. But like I said, it's not always our choice. We loved being back home and spending time with our family, but this move would only be the continuation of a journey that took us back and forth across the country, wherever God led us. We didn't always understand the moves, and maybe we didn't always make the right decisions. But, we knew God was always by our side and making something special happen everywhere we travelled, constantly nudging us toward the correct path. We tried to find a reason why He would take us each place. But He never left us any notes to confirm our hunches. Regardless of how difficult it was to pick up and leave time after time, we believed God would somehow lead us back—back to the family I loved so deeply.

We moved to Maine in January of 2009 and stayed for one year. I loved it there. Yes, it was cold, and yes, it snowed a lot. It snowed twenty-two inches the day after we moved in; welcome! But there were also lots of fun things to do. We took trips as a family to Acadia National Park. We saw lighthouses and went whale watching. Maine is a one-of-a-kind state, so different from anywhere else we lived. Charles enjoyed working as general manager at a country club, and things were going well. But nine months in, as he worked on the budget he saw this club was in serious financial trouble. They would not listen to his ideas on how to get out of it, as the club was run by board members who seemed to think they knew better. One of the most brilliant parts of Charles is that he knows when to put up a fight and when it is fruitless. He decided on preemptive resumes. He was not going to wait for the ship to go down. He truly believed this club would go under. It was a shame because it was beautiful and had a great family atmosphere. I could see myself staying there forever. But it was not meant to be.

I can't say I ever figured out why we moved to Maine. I started to feel we might just be meant to be wanderers, never truly settling anywhere. When we trust in God's will, we don't get to pick our path; He chooses it for us. But that doesn't make it any easier.

I was not prepared, however, for the location of Charles's next *"I got an interview"* reveal. It was Arizona this time. Again with the cross-country journey? This time, if there was a silver lining, it was that this company's headquarters were in Philadelphia. If he put in the time, there was an opportunity to return to Pennsylvania to work in the corporate sector. This scenario seemed promising. It was a breathtaking location—Lake Powell. It was also an extremely remote area, two hours from anywhere. That really didn't bother us much because we were an adventurous couple and up for the challenge.

Charles received a call less than a week after he returned from his interview. The offer was there, and now it was our decision to take it or leave it. We never made immediate decisions, but always talked these opportunities through. When we both felt it was the right direction for our family, after a time of prayer we embraced the new reality. This time we headed for the desert. Moving is very difficult, but it also has its positives. Starting over new is exciting if you have the right attitude, and like I said, this seemed to be our new normal; so why not have some fun on the ride?

We spent nearly two and a half years in Arizona. It was a new record for the length of time in one place since Canyon came along. We made a lot of great memories. Yet, with the good times we also experienced devastation. During this time out west, we had two miscarriages. We wanted so badly to have another child, but with each passing year it seemed less and less likely. It was so hard to comprehend that after having a smooth nine-month pregnancy with Canyon, these latest pregnancies were going so very wrong almost immediately.

I didn't smoke or drink; I ate a healthy diet and exercised, so it was difficult to understand why it was happening. We never planned on having an only child, but the reality of it started creeping in the back of our minds. Plus, the pain of our losses was monumentally more difficult each time. We continued to pray that if it be God's will, we would have another child. All we could do was trust.

Overall, our time in Arizona was wonderful, new, and exciting. However, our hopeful plans of returning east seemed to fizzle before our eyes in the coming months. The winds of change were on the horizon again, and putting down roots here was not part of the plan. The gusts were blowing in a different direction entirely.

***

Understanding. I prayed for it continuously, but many times it did not come. Throughout the years, many family members and friends could not comprehend why we moved so often. Welcome to our world; neither did we! Sometimes that is the difficulty in praying for God's will; it does not always line up with ours, and consequently life can get tough. Confusion ensues. But His promises are true, and His plans are good. We believed that would be true for us.

> *Jesus replied, "You don't understand now what I am doing, but someday you will" (John 13:7).*

CHAPTER 13

THE LOOK

TUESDAY, JUNE 28th 2016, THE HOSPITAL

The procedure to put in the new PICC line for Mom would take over an hour, so, again, we had nothing to do but wait. I don't know how we managed to fill all our time that day. I guess we looked at magazines, made small talk, and stared at the wall. I know we prayed a lot, but the rest of the day was sort of a blur. I did take time to talk with a few of Mom's friends during the wait about her cancer diagnosis. In all this chaos, it was so secondary, but the truth was if she got better, she still had cancer. We knew what kind and what stage, but Mom was still waiting to find out if it was an aggressive cancer, which is something she was anxious to know. Of course, none of her friends knew about her diagnosis yet, as she just found out the day before. They did, however, know about the nutritional products she was taking for the last two years and how much she believed in them. I briefly filled them in on the plan we discussed, which included changing her diet, the water she drank, and at the core of the plan, the products. Her friends undoubtedly saw the change in her from taking this nutrition in the last twenty-four months, but using them to treat cancer? I am confident they never heard of such a thing.

Nobody said too much about it but from comments Mom would receive later, I know that many of them probably had the same thoughts. She should have surgery, get radiation, and go the traditional route. It worked for others they knew. But they didn't say anything negative at the time, and I appreciated that. Why be pessimistic when she is still in critical condition? They were here to support my mom, and it was nice to have them around to lean on.

Finally, a nurse came in and told us everything went fine with the new line, which was a relief. There was now more insurance as to how well they could help her in the event of another crisis.

"She's had some pretty nasty stuff put in her body to keep her alive," the nurse explained.

I hated to hear all her body was going through, along with having cancer, but none of that mattered at this point. Short term goals were what we were after, getting her off the breathing machine and finding a cause for what went so wrong that it caused sudden cardiac death.

Dave finally left to get something to eat with Pat, so Justin and I headed back in to sit by Mom's side. The nurses told us she was awake. We saw the doctor in the hallway and asked what we should say to her about what happened. This was all so new to us.

"Just tell her she passed out, and she is okay now. Keep it simple," he suggested.

We took our same positions by her sides, and I got a chance to see the beauty of her bright blue eyes for the first time that day. I can't describe the feeling very well, but it was almost breathtaking. You can't truly appreciate something so simple like seeing your mother's eyes until it's taken away. I relished every second of it. I tried hard to keep my composure. As I mentioned, Mom can read me like a book, and I wanted her to see that everything was all right when she looked at me. I am about the worst faker in history. But I wasn't going to have to lie because she was okay right now, so I felt fine telling her that. You could see the confusion on her face the moment she saw us. Her face was contorted, and she was searching her memory for why she was here but getting nothing.

"You passed out at home, and they brought you to the hospital. Everything is okay now," I assured her.

I stroked her face and told her to just rest; that was all she needed to do. You could see the tension in her face subside, and she closed her eyes. Justin and I sat back in our chairs for the next few minutes to just enjoy seeing her awake. We could tell she was so tired; her body was begging for some sleep. The ease of that next five minutes was erased as she again awoke with the same troubled expression, looking for an answer as to why she was in this bed with something stuck down her throat. This look would be forever ingrained in my brain. I was not used to seeing her so helpless.

"It's okay, Mom," Justin now took a turn. "You passed out at home making Dave's lunch this morning, and they brought you here. Everything is okay."

Her confusion was relieved again and back to sleep she went. The only problem? She would do this same thing close to fifteen times in the next hour or so.

"Dear God, please don't let her have brain damage. This *cannot* be her life," I prayed.

We were so glad she came back to us, but lacking a short-term memory was not going to be any quality of life she would want. My mom was used to being on top of every detail. She was so organized and reliable in everything she did. She just had to get better. Thankfully, God gave Justin and me the strength to continually tell the story without breaking down. Dave, on the other hand, could not handle it as this scenario continued throughout the day. After everything he did to save her, watching her like this was gut wrenching.

"It's fine," I told him, "we will stay with her. You *need* to take some breaks."

I couldn't even begin to think about what he went through that day; seeing her like this was potentially enough to send him over the edge. I was so grateful to him and didn't want that to happen. I was more than happy to stay by her side and thankful that I now lived close enough to help. There was no place else I wanted to be anyway, not even for a moment.

Justin had to eventually go home to his wife and four children for a short while. I continued to stare at Mom's blood pressure numbers, willing them to go up. It wasn't working, and I finally asked a nurse if the numbers were a concern. He assured me the doctors were happy with them. What? How could they be? He explained that compared to where she had been all day, these numbers weren't bad. They had not changed in hours and seemed so low to me. But I was amazed that many conditions that would normally be unacceptable were considered to be an improvement. I tried to relax, but it was impossible.

Mom awoke a few more times, and I repeated the story to her. One time the doctor came back to check on her, and I saw her stare toward him for clarification. He told her the same story, but this time she still seemed a little confused as she looked in his direction. And then it hit me. First, not only is she at a loss about what happened and why she has something stuck down her throat, but she may not even be able to see. I asked her if she put her contacts in that morning, and she shook her head. It was such a small thing, but she was listening and understanding my question. It made me so happy. I relayed to the doctor that without her contacts she was blind as a bat, and he needed to get closer to her while talking. It made a big difference the next few times we told her. I thought she was so confused because she didn't know why she was in this room, but the truth is she probably had no idea where she was because her world was completely fuzzy. I made a mental note to text Dave to bring her glasses. I wanted to do anything that might make her feel better immediately. It didn't make her remember the details for any length of time. But, the doctor would mention during his final visit of the night that this type of memory loss was normal. He wasn't concerned yet. So, I did my best not to be either. I was failing, but I kept on trying.

Mom seemed to be staying awake a little longer each time she opened her eyes. The doctor continued to check on her vitals and said in the next hour or two he was going to take her off the ventilator. This was phenomenal news! Think about it. Twelve hours ago, she was dead for over forty minutes, and now she made such a turnaround she could breathe on her own. You don't usually get notification of a miracle in progress, but I knew I was watching one happen with each passing hour. She was a warrior with a God-led army that was mowing down her obstacles. He was breathing life back into her minute by minute.

***

Prayer warriors are people who are known for regularly interceding on behalf of others before God. Sometimes I have heard people say they don't pray as well as others they know. Never believe that. There are no special skills needed to lift your voice up to Heaven. I saw first-hand how crucial each and every prayer from a believer can be, and I will never be able to thank those people enough. Use your power from God each and every day.

For where two or three gather together as my followers, I am there among them (Matthew 18:20).

CHAPTER 14

THE LONE STAR STATE

NOVEMBER 2011, ARIZONA

For the first year and a half in Arizona, we lived by Lake Powell. Charles managed the large resort that sat on its shores. It was an expansive place and he was kept busy. He liked the job but noticed quickly that his boss's management style did not match his own. We've learned through the years that the personality you see in a potential boss in an interview does not always match the personality out of the interview. But there is nothing you can do about it. Charles's theory was to surround himself with good people and then let them do their jobs. This was completely opposite of this boss. He was a micro-manager and smothered everyone constantly, but Charles did his best to deal with it.

As year two was approaching, though, the clash of personalities was becoming more of an issue, and we talked about it several times. We didn't think there was much to do about it in the short term. We were in the middle of nowhere, and there weren't any other jobs to even apply for that didn't mean packing up again. And then, there was one.

Charles continued working and making the best of it, as the area we lived in was amazing, and there was no reason to rush anything. A few months later, though, a job posting caught his eye. It was an opportunity based out of the town we lived in, but it was to manage the Grand Canyon. The canyon was closed in the wintertime and two hours away, so the manager would stay in town during the off season. We wouldn't even have to move.

The company's president flew into town a few weeks later, and Charles got a chance to sit down with him. They liked his resume and his experience working in remote places. They needed someone who could thrive at a place so secluded. Bingo. They had found the right man and the right family. It was good timing for the transition because the season was already over at the Grand Canyon, so Charles could work from town for the next six months. We could figure out the summer season later.

The men from this company had the same approach to business Charles did, and it was wonderful. They knew he had the experience to be successful, and they put their trust in him to do so. As the reopening of the park approached, we decided as a family to move to the Grand Canyon with him so he wouldn't spend so much time commuting back and forth. It was only two hours away, which was nothing for us as far as moving. We had a huge sale and got rid of almost all of our furniture. We were going from a house to small employee accommodations, but we didn't care. We knew it would be a once-in-a-lifetime experience for Canyon. And by the way, how unbelievable is it that we ended up living at the place Canyon was named after, even though we came up with the name while living in Pennsylvania? Kind of cool, right?

It was a summer to remember. Canyon and I explored the area nearly every day while Charles was working, and we took family hikes at night. We enjoyed eating lunch with Charles in the lodge that had a view of the Grand Canyon. It is one of the most spectacular sites on earth—just phenomenal to see in person. Canyon thrived, and we knew he had our genes and love of the outdoors. Charles had a wonderful summer, and as it began to wind down we felt like it was a win for all of us. As much as we loved it, though, we had to start looking at the future, because Canyon was now five and needed to be in school soon. We decided to wait on kindergarten until the next year, but we were going to have to head for civilization in the coming months. The Grand Canyon left us with some one-of-a-kind memories, and we will always be grateful to that company for the opportunity. Fortunately, they had hotels in other states that Charles could transfer to at the end of that season, and one of these options would mean going back to Charles's roots. We hadn't tried the southern part of the United States, so why not? We moved east once for my family, so we felt the pull to go closer to those he loved for a change. We were grateful that Canyon would get to know Charles's side of the family, so the decision was made. Next stop—the Lone Star State.

***

Where we lived began to matter less and less to us. Clearly, we were not destined for a stationary life. God had us on the move again, and we trusted in Him completely. We went wherever He sent us, hoping to do His will with each location choice we made.

> *You love him even though you have never seen him. Though you do not see him now, you trust him; and you rejoice with a glorious, inexpressible joy. The reward for trusting him will be the salvation of your souls (1 Peter 1:8-9).*

CHAPTER 15

THE SOUND

TUESDAY, JUNE 28th 2016, THE HOSPITAL

Justin returned to the hospital that evening, and I told him that Mom would be off the ventilator soon. He was ecstatic. We were both in our usual spots with Mom resting comfortably when I noticed her sit up quickly. She had not made any sudden movements up to this point, so of course it concerned me. My concern kicked into sheer panic as I saw her face go beet red in an instant, and she looked at me wild-eyed and afraid. She couldn't breathe.

"She's *choking*!" I screamed and bolted into the hallway. "She's choking, choking, choking!" I repeated in a voice my brother would later say was louder than necessary, in his opinion.

The nurse made his way in, but not quickly enough in my view. As I turned back to my mom, she was still red, but the nurse very calmly let her know it was fine. She was just coughing, and it happens all the time. Okay, I would have appreciated a little heads up on the subject. Maybe some sort of pamphlet, or perhaps a post-it note regarding ventilators and this coughing possibility, along with the appropriate reaction to it. Choking and coughing are completely different, and I couldn't tell what was happening. Justin, on the other hand, never moved the entire time.

I turned to him. "How in the world are you just sitting there? I thought she was dying!"

He was back to his calm self by this point in the day, and in a very matter-of-fact voice said if she was dying, he thought someone would come to help. You see, this is why I am not known as the eye of a hurricane. Luckily, I was not escorted from the ICU immediately, and later, much later, as I would retell the story to Mom we all had a good laugh about it.

I did not see anyone laughing at that point, however. I just knew from that day forward every time I came to her room there would be whispers of, "There she is. Can you believe that girl screamed at the top of her lungs in the ICU?"

Yes, okay, my bad. But, come on, I was having a tough day and just slightly on edge. An hour later, we could all rest easy as the tube was taken out, and she was breathing like a champ. I'm sure there was a collective sigh of relief among all medical staff working on the floor that no more outbursts were forthcoming. As we reentered the room, Mom looked at us and smiled.

"Hi," she said.

But it wasn't just hearing her voice that made me beam like a Cheshire cat; it was the actual tone of it. My mom normally has a low speaking voice, but the pitch that came out of her was so foreign. It sounded like she just sucked on a helium balloon in the moments prior. The doctor said it was a side effect of the breathing tube, but for me it added some much-needed levity after such a difficult day. We all know how funny it is to hear someone talk on helium, but it usually only lasts a short time. This effect, however, would continue for the next day, and it was the cutest thing ever. She, of course, had no idea it was happening, which made it even better.

We could give her some more details of the day's events, and she was shocked each time we went through it. She would eventually ask again. What day is this? What happened? Dave had to do what? But the sweetest part each time was when we would end the story.

As soon as we concluded, she would immediately say, "I can't die, I have grandbabies!" in a voice I could only to attribute to that of a cartoon character.

To be able to smile again on this day was a joy that could not be measured. I would have never guessed it would be from hearing my mom sound so comical, but hey, I'm not complaining. Later that night when I was alone in the room, a hospital chaplain came in. She told my mom she was the talk of the hospital. Everyone knew about the woman who survived what seemed like the impossible, and news of her miraculous recovery was widespread.

"Me, really?" Mom squeaked.

None of the information she was being given was really sinking in at this point. She didn't seem to understand what all the fuss was about. It was precious.

As I filled the chaplain in on some of the details of the day, my mom looked at her and said joyfully, "I can't die, I have grandbabies!"

"Exactly," the chaplain replied, "you're right, you can't."

We all chatted for a few more minutes, although the chaplain and I did most of the talking because I told Mom she was advised by the doctor not to talk very much. Her vocal chords were inflamed, and they needed time to heal.

"Can I pray with you?" the chaplain asked.

My mom nodded, trying to take the advice not to talk. The chaplain thanked God for all that happened that day. She spoke of His perfect timing and the work of the doctors, along with the healing that took place.

In the middle of the prayer, she continued by giving praise that Mom made it through, to which Mom interrupted squeakily, no longer able to contain herself, "I can't die, I have grandbabies!"

I don't know what was funnier, the fact that Mom interjected in her high-pitched voice during someone else's prayer, when she was never someone who interrupted others, or that the chaplain kept a straight face.

She replied, "Yeeesssss, I've heard that somewhere before."

That is one prayer I will never forget, but it was clear Mom loved her grandchildren—of that there was no doubt. At close to 9 p.m., the doctor came in one last time and told us they finally got word of the EKG results. Although they would never be able to definitively say, their best guess was that Mom had an electrical malfunction of her heart.

"Some people just have extra beats that are unexplained," he said. "There are those who have a lot—ten, twenty, or more each minute. Your mom only has a few. Normally there is nothing dangerous about it. Her heart in general looks okay; she just got extremely unlucky and two of her beats hit at the exact same time. When the two beats collide, the heart just stops working, almost immediately. It's very rare something like this happens. Almost a one in a million shot."

He related it to being like a short circuit. He said when this happens, it is usually fatal. We would learn later the statistics on these types of electrical problems. Only seven percent of people who have them outside of a hospital survive. This was another detail I was thankful to learn later as the 50-50 chance she seemed to have that morning was already enough for all of us to have a breakdown.

The start and finish to this day felt as if there was a lifetime in between. We were all emotionally and physically exhausted, but God was good, and Mom was alive. Fourteen hours later it seemed okay to go get some rest. We all knew who was in control here, and His plans for my mom were not close to being finished.

***

To hear my mom's voice after she came so close to death was a joy that could never be measured. I admit my weakness throughout this day, but seeing her smiling face again taught me an invaluable lesson. We should expect God to move, not just hope for it. We should not pray thinking it is better than doing nothing. We should know our prayers are on a direct line to Him at all times, and He answers all that come in His will.

> But in my distress I cried out to the Lord; yes, I prayed to my God for help. He heard me from his sanctuary; my cry to him reached his ears (Psalms 18:6).

CHAPTER 16

THE STINT

OCTOBER 2012, TEXAS

The hotel Charles managed in Texas was outside of Dallas. We decided for the first time to try a neighborhood, so Canyon could be around more children, and were happy with the home we found. The back yard was a bit of an adjustment as it was very small, and we could see five other homes around us. It was not exactly the nature we were used to, but learning to adjust was becoming a strength of ours. We tried to show our son how to be positive in whatever situation you find yourself in. But adjusting was not much of a strength for Canyon yet. He was an amazing child, but slightly introverted, so constantly meeting new people was not his thing, even though it was all he knew. We were starting to feel badly about moving him so much, but we also did our best to show him the value of new experiences.

We found a preschool we really liked, and Canyon started immediately because it was already October. The nice thing about being new is that kids always gravitate toward you. Canyon is also an extremely kind child, and the students loved him right away. He began to settle in, and we all did our best to adjust to culture shock. Instead of the Grand Canyon, we were now engulfed by stores, restaurants, and traffic lights.

When you get so used to a certain way of living, change is hard. Yet, that was part of what I embraced about the frequency of our moves. I felt we were growing in lots of different ways. We met so many unique people along the way and had to adapt to each situation. I believe all the families we met had something to teach us. I just hoped that we also were a positive light in their lives.

While in Texas, we could spend more time with Charles's family because they lived within a half an hour. His mom and I took Canyon on a train to a museum in downtown Dallas, and it was fun to do something so totally different. Canyon also got to experience the "Jerry Jones effect" when we took him to the Cowboys' stadium one weekend. The crazy thing is, even though I grew up in Pennsylvania, for some reason I always loved the Dallas Cowboys, and so did Charles. I think it's required for Texans. Inevitably, Canyon had no other choice but to be a super fan, and he loved every second of being there. Cities have their own unique benefits, and getting to go to major-league sporting events was something Canyon always remembered. We also spent time watching the baseball team the Texas Rangers play during our stint.

Why the word *stint*? Because that's what it ended up feeling like.

Although it was extremely hot and not really our type of area, we were making it work just like we always tried to do. Because he was away from Texas for such an extended period, even Charles no longer enjoyed the weather or the traffic. We were used to wide open spaces and not being able to touch the house next to us. Yet, his family was close, and his job was good. Canyon liked his school and new friends. We had lots of play dates and special routines we were establishing. We were just going with the flow, no real long-term plans, but no plans to make any moves any time soon.

Are you picking up my foreshadowing? We had established a pattern by this time, and it was not a pattern of staying.

Luckily, I hadn't unpacked all our boxes at this point, because we had only lived near Dallas about six months when Charles's company was bought out. With a new owner comes new management, because they choose their own people. It's just a given. Charles always told me it was part of the risk of the hospitality field, because hotels are sold all the time, but it was not something we had experienced so far. There was a first time for everything, so here we were.

What was difficult about the sudden change was that part of us felt this move close to a big city was God's way of getting us to a specialist to help us have another child. Whenever we felt like we might possibly be in on God's secret plans, it always made the move seem a little more worth it. There was an extra excitement in the air for us as we thought we finally caught on. We went to see a specialist in those first six months and she performed every test possible to see what was happening. The doctor was surprised we had been pregnant four times at this point. Even though I was only in my mid 30s, she said I had the eggs of an older woman, and that combined with an underactive thyroid left our chances of getting pregnant on our own at one to three percent. That was not encouraging, but we had come seeking answers. We believed with the specialist's help, we could be successful with a full-term pregnancy.

She suggested we try IUI, intrauterine insemination. This advice was a lot to take in, but she was the expert, and if that's what it took then we were willing to try. There was some preparation for this procedure, but we started the process and were excited about the possibilities. However, the week before it was scheduled, she said I had cysts on my ovaries, and she would be unable to do it. At this point, we'd have to wait until that cleared up, and it could take months. It was upsetting, and in my heart I kept wondering if it was ever going to happen. From what the doctor said, not only did we have a problem sustaining a pregnancy, but we had little chance going forward of even getting pregnant without help. We never had another chance to have the procedure done, as our short stay was already about to be over.

The other tough part of such a sudden change was that the process of finding a new job in Charles's line of work usually took a minimum of two months. Usually, there would be hundreds of applicants and at least three interviews. He didn't plan on searching for anything else, so all we could do was hunker down in Texas and wait as his resumes were being reviewed. This was the first time we felt a bit stuck and confused about the way things unfolded. Our pregnancy theory was obviously wrong, so why were we here? Honestly, I never really felt like I had a guess, but it didn't matter because times like this confirmed we were a strong family. God brought us together in a way only He could arrange, and we were grateful. I read once that job changes and moves are some of the biggest stresses in a marriage and high on the reasons for divorce. But here we were ready for move number seven. We had each other, and that was all that mattered.

After a few months of resumes, Charles had two jobs he was interviewing for. It was an interesting crossroads. One opportunity was in Myrtle Beach, South Carolina and the other in Las Vegas, Nevada. As I mentioned, the interview process was extensive, and each place did things in their own timing. The Myrtle Beach job was one step ahead of the Vegas job, which posed a bit of a problem. Charles had already been for the onsite interview in South Carolina, with a trip scheduled to Nevada the following week. The other issue was the type of job being offered. The Myrtle Beach position was for a general manager at a resort, while the Vegas job was a higher-level position as a regional vice president. It meant a lot more money, but also more travel and a much greater distance from my family. We would be near my older brother Ryan, which was something to consider. There was no way to make this decision on our own, and we were glad to take it out of our hands and give it to God. Being human means you make mistakes, and even though we always prayed and thought we were doing our best to listen to God, we never fully know if we have made the right choice. So, there was no question we were not going to just wing it.

Ultimately, Charles was offered the job in South Carolina, and we decided we weren't going to chance losing that opportunity to stall for another interview in Vegas. We also felt the money to head back west was not worth it. We didn't want him traveling and missing out on family time. We were going to check off another landscape to our list. We had done the mountains, the desert, and the flat lands of Texas. The beach seemed like a logical next step on our God-led journey. There are not enough words to express how thankful I am that God made that choice clear for us, because this move would not only affect our lives but the life of my mom years before I would know how badly she'd need it.

***

Making assumptions can always get us in trouble. Thinking we had even an inkling into God's plans was foolish. But turning to Him in our confusion was the smartest thing we could have done. There were no flashing lights saying "greatness ahead," but heeding that small whisper that nudges you in a certain direction has power to move a mountain, although unseen.

> *Rejoice in our confident hope. Be patient in trouble, and keep on praying (Romans 12:12).*

CHAPTER 17

THE TRANSITION

WENESDAY, JUNE 29th 2016, PENNSYLVANIA

I stayed with my grandmother that first night to keep her company. I know she didn't need to have me there. She is a very strong and independent lady, but I sort of wanted to be with her, so maybe it was more me wanting her comfort. As she was eating her breakfast the next morning, I asked if she cared if I headed over to hospital while she finished up. I was so antsy to see my mom. Mimi didn't mind, so I headed straight for the door.

The doctors asked us not to visit before 9 a.m. because we wouldn't be able to see her while rounds were going on. When I arrived, I immediately saw Dave in the hallway, and he did not look good. My heart sank. I wished I never left because this was exactly what I was afraid of—something happening when I wasn't there.

"What's wrong?" I asked frantically.

He looked as if he hadn't slept, which was confusing. I thought things were just fine when we left last night. Everything was headed in the right direction. Maybe this is why doctors refused to use the word "stable." I almost couldn't bear to look in Mom's room. I braced myself and took a quick peek. She looked like she was sleeping comfortably. What was going on? Was she paralyzed again? Was she unconscious? *What*? I felt my body panic.

Dave quickly explained because he could tell I was about to lose it. "She's fine. I got a call from my brother Gary at 5 a.m. because someone posted online to pray for your mom. They said she was headed for an emergency surgery to save her life. Gary called asking what happened to cause such a drastic change. I had no idea what he was talking about so I jumped in my truck and raced down here, scared to death!"

This is where we learned a valuable lesson about social media. It was a wonderful tool to spread the word quickly and have lots of people praying for my mom. But when someone reposted the original post at 5 a.m. the next morning, asking people to pray for her lifesaving surgery because they hadn't seen the updates, chaos ensues. Poor Dave. Thankfully, he wasn't in any sort of accident on the way to the hospital and did not have his own heart issues as he raced to Mom's side!

His fears were put to rest when he got to the hospital, but it took a toll on him in the process. Mom was still doing very well, and there was nothing to worry about. However, it meant he had already been here four hours and was wrecked. He had been unable to get more than about thirty minutes rest that night anyway. There was just too much going on for him to sleep soundly. When he had finally made it home that night, he walked into a scene that was haunting.

There was dried blood on the kitchen tile where Mom had been lying. Food was still on the counter where she had placed it to make his lunch. The "*what ifs*" were difficult to think about. He tried to piece together exactly how the scene played out.

From where she ended up on the floor, he realized Mom was making him a salad that day. There was lettuce on the counter by the stove. She must have needed something else from the refrigerator because the door was still open when he first found her. The vision of her replayed in his mind. He could still see the angle of her body lying so helpless, the gray color of her skin, and her position that left a bloody stain on the tile. She must have hit her head on the counter on the way down because of where she was standing in front of the refrigerator. We got word that morning that the cut on her head already closed on its own without treatment. Again, it was an amazing bit of healing in such a short amount of time. We were all so thankful about that, but Dave had another reason to be grateful as he thought back to when he and Mom put those counters in. One of those nudges that had him suggest something that may have changed Mom's prognosis.

It was a few years previously when they decided to do some renovations—new floors, new paint, and a new island that separated the kitchen from the living room. By this time, there were already a few grandchildren who would run around during visits to the house. I still remember how proud my mom was of Dave at his recommendation to make rounded corners for the island instead of squared edges. It was a last-minute change from what they originally discussed.

"He said the more he thought about it, he doesn't want any of the kids to have the possibility of getting injured running into the sharp edge and hurting their heads," Mom beamed. "Isn't that the sweetest thing you've ever heard, that he would think of such a thing?"

Yes, it was. I certainly hadn't thought about it. To this day only one person has hit their head on the counter's edge, and it wasn't one of the kids. How different might things be if Mom fell into a squared edge without any chance of bracing herself? What if there were no grandchildren around so Dave never considered that change in plans? I have a feeling it wouldn't have been a wound that could close on its own after only one day. Thankfully, we never had to find out what could have been, but it was just one more sign of God's hand protecting her years in advance. These small wonders were sprinkled everywhere in my mom's story, and there are not enough words to describe my gratitude.

Back at the hospital, I pleaded with Dave to go home and try to sleep as I was now here for the duration of the day and he didn't have to worry. He finally obliged. When I snuck in the room, Mom was asleep, so I just took a seat and held her hand again. I decided to take a different side of the bed that day and face the window, so I couldn't see the blood pressure numbers. They were still low, and I didn't like them, so I tried to ignore them. She was starting to sleep longer and more comfortably the longer the breathing tube was out. I was glad her body was working on regaining the strength she needed to really turn a corner. I stayed with her all morning as she dozed in and out, and when she awoke I went through the story just like yesterday. Each time she heard it she was just as surprised. It was an amazing story, so I could understand why it would be so overwhelming. She was getting a little frustrated that she couldn't remember anything, but I tried to reassure her it was normal. I was hoping as I assured her it would start sinking in for me too. But, at least now we knew the gouge on the back of her head was not a big deal and not adding to any brain issues.

Justin took a break from work at lunchtime and came by. Mom's face lit up when she saw him. They went through the familiar "what happened to me" scenario like she did with each new person that came in the room. We were becoming accustomed to it, but obviously did not want it to be the new normal. There were lots of people still coming to the waiting room, but we weren't letting anyone but family see her. I know my mom well enough that she wouldn't want anybody seeing her in this condition. Although it was an amazing change, she still wasn't herself. And though everything about her resonated beauty to me, I realized she would not agree if she looked in a mirror. It was an easy decision—no visitors that day.

The doctor came in with his updates, and her situation was encouraging. Her vitals had looked good all through the night. They felt confident in their assessment of what caused the problem, and the solution was to put in a defibrillator. It was basically an internal shocker that would put her heart back in its normal rhythm if this was to ever happen again. This would be like an added insurance policy. She needed to be stable for a few days before they could consider putting it in, because it was another procedure to put her body through. She would also need to be transferred to another hospital because they did not put defibrillators in at this one. But, he was extremely pleased with her progress, and was already considering moving her out of the ICU later that day. What a difference a day can make! The next few hours we just waited and prayed she would make the transition to the step-down floor.

The afternoon came and went without incident, and her blood pressure numbers were beginning to creep up, finally. She was in very good spirits for someone who had gone through so much the day before. And to see her spirits high was all we needed to be in good moods ourselves. Even with all that had happened, I was starting to see that joy in my mom, a quality I knew not everyone could exude this quickly after such a tragic event. We hadn't yet given her too many details on how long she was dead, and she was still on so much medication that she wouldn't feel the effects of all the CPR until days later, when she could really piece the story together.

When Dave returned a few hours later, we got more good news. The oncologist's office called and confirmed that her cancer was non-aggressive. Hallelujah! Cancer is such a frightening disease, and it was still in the back of my mind that any time she was not actively treating the cancer, it could be growing, especially if it was aggressive. A week can sometimes make a big difference, and at this point they seemed to think that's how long her total stay might end up being. I was afraid to think about what might be happening in her body during that time. We couldn't change how long she'd be here, but this news was the best-case scenario at that point.

Mom and I talked extensively on Monday about her plans to take the nutrition and flood her body with it to treat her cancer. She was going to be drinking six shakes a day—about one every two and a half hours. Yet, up to this point no one even mentioned cancer to my mom, and Dave relayed the phone call details to Justin and me in private. We wanted her to only think about getting better, and we weren't going to put any more stress on her body.

By dinner time, the news we were waiting to hear was delivered. She was moving to step down. It's funny because step down is literally just down the hall and through a set of double doors, but it seemed a lifetime away from what it meant to be in the ICU. Deep breaths could be taken, sighs of relief seemed acceptable and permanent smiles on our faces were appropriate. Life was good, knowing my favorite woman on this earth was going to be okay.

After she settled in for a little while, they brought her the first meal she would be allowed in the hospital. I was just walking back into the room when I saw it. I'm not going to lie, I was a little shocked at their choice—meatloaf and mashed potatoes. For real? For a woman who had just come off a breathing tube the night before, this is what you find most appropriate? As I began a mini rant on the poor choice, Justin let me know that it was a mix up and her "sandwich" was on its way, eventually. Mom was too hungry to wait, so she dug in. But after a few bites, she became quickly uninterested. I don't blame her. Hospital meatloaf—yuck. Justin gave her the other options from the plate, and the only thing she said sounded good was the fruit. For the next fifteen minutes, I watched one of the sweetest scenes ever as Justin spoon fed her every bite and she "*Hmmmmed*" the whole way through it. She said it hit the spot, and it made me smile to watch Justin add such a personal touch to her day. But that is his thing, knowing just what to do and when to do it.

Dave, Justin, and I visited with her a little while longer, and then Dave headed home and Justin followed closely behind, as he had to work the next day. We all wanted her to have an early night, so we weren't going to stay late again. She wanted to watch a little TV and fall asleep to it, because that was her normal routine at home. I was happy to oblige, and turned it on because all I wanted for her was to get back to what was normal. I crawled in bed with her, and just relished listening to her breathing get heavier as she started nodding off. Day two at the hospital was in the books, and as hospital days go, it was fantastic all around.

> *Then you will experience God's peace, which exceeds anything we can understand. His peace will guard your hearts and minds as you live in Christ Jesus (Philippians 4:7).*

CHAPTER 18

THE BEACH

OCTOBER 2012, MYRTLE BEACH, SC

Living at the beach was a wonderful change of pace. Canyon loved the ocean, and through Charles's work we instantly had some connections with other families, many of whom had boys Canyon's age. We spent lots of time at the ocean that summer, and it seemed to be a smooth transition for Canyon this time. He was immediately invited to birthday parties and got to know kids on his sports teams, so we were pleased with everything. Charles also seemed to enjoy his job.

In March of that first year living in South Carolina, we got a big surprise. We were pregnant again! Charles and I hadn't even discussed the baby aspect since we arrived because the moving process was so consuming, and life just started getting busy. Because of what the specialist told us, we didn't consider the possibility that I might become pregnant accidently. We certainly weren't trying to be careful as there didn't seem to be a need. As a couple who had tried to get pregnant every month for over three years, I guess not thinking about it for once helped. People would always tell me to just put it out of my mind, and we would get pregnant. These were people, though, who got pregnant easily, so that wasn't as simple as they wanted it to be for me. But, we were pregnant and we were thrilled. I immediately found a doctor and begged to get the earliest appointment I could. I was seen the next day and told we were about six weeks pregnant. This was about the time I always seemed to miscarry, so it was nerve wracking. The doctor put me on some extra supplements because I filled her in on my history, and we prayed they would help.

At eight weeks, Charles and I went back for an ultrasound. With the issues we had, the doctor wanted to see me every two weeks in the beginning, which was fine by me. It helped ease my fears. We got to hear the baby's heartbeat, and I think we both teared up at the sound. We never heard the heartbeat of the other three babies, so this was very encouraging. She said the baby looked great, and I should come back in another two weeks. We were feeling good about this pregnancy and began to allow ourselves the happiness that came with it. We were past our normal point of miscarriage, and with our healthy report from the doctor we felt we could share the news with Canyon. He never knew of any of our other losses.

There had been so many times over the years when he asked for a sibling, and it was so hard to just keep assuring him we were trying. When he was about four he kept asking me where babies came from and why weren't we having one? I finally just blurted out that mommies and daddies need to hug and kiss a lot to have a child. He seemed satisfied, thank goodness. But since that time, we were encouraged by him on many occasions to start hugging and kissing a lot more so he could get a brother. It was so sweet but also heartbreaking.

Canyon was beyond excited to hear the news. We began to talk about how great it would be, having someone who would adore him more than he could imagine. He would have someone to play with and share secrets with—all the wonderful parts of having a sibling. The future was exciting. Canyon and I travelled to Pennsylvania on spring break a short time later, and we also decided to share the news with the family because I was at ten weeks by now. I felt good, and we had a wonderful time while we were there. I also convinced my mom to come back with us and spend some time in Myrtle Beach. I sweetened the pot by letting her know I had another ultrasound coming up, and she could come to my appointment and see the baby. That did it; she was coming.

Having her along made the twelve-hour trip much more enjoyable, and we talked the whole way. With Canyon back in school on Monday,

Charles and I, along with my mom, headed to my eleven-week appointment. We chatted with the doctor briefly, and then she got out the ultrasound machine. They had a big screen on the wall, and she told us to look up there for the baby. The doctor began to move her wand around to bring up the picture. It took me less than a minute to know something was wrong. I was watching her expression closely. I could not see Charles as he was behind me, but I knew my mom was looking at the screen in anticipation, so she didn't notice. The doctor's face seemed to pinch up, and I stared at her as she squinted to get a closer look at the screen. For the next few minutes she searched, but I already turned my head away. I knew.

She didn't have to say a word but she did anyway: "I am so sorry, but I can't find a heartbeat."

"What?" I heard my Mom ask, incredulous. She just knew she heard that wrong.

"The baby's gone," I repeated to her.

I wish I could say I was just as shocked as she was, but when you've lost three babies already, there is always a fear that is impossible to deny completely. My mom's facial expression was indescribable. If it was possible, she seemed to be in more pain than I was. It was taking over her body. I still couldn't see Charles, but my mom would tell me later that she would never forget the look on his face, which I am sort of glad I couldn't see. It would have made everything hurt so much more. Looking at the man who was always the pillar of strength in our family and seeing a pain that deep would put me at even more of a loss. He has always been the one to be strong during our difficulties, always pointing to God and His plans for us. His words of encouragement were always about having faith and trusting in our path, even when we didn't understand it. And there had been much we didn't understand through the years. But I know losing a fourth child shocked him to the core, and now we had to tell Canyon.

Canyon's cries when he heard the news were like a knife to the heart. We wanted to find a way to make it okay, but we couldn't. He is a sensitive boy and his pain was so raw that he just let it out, over and over. We just sat with him and held him tight while he cried. Every time we thought he was done, he would start up again. It was like our words would replay in his mind, and a new wave of pain hit him, and he would start to wail. We felt so guilty that we had told him. Being a parent can be so difficult sometimes, and even the best of intentions can have terrible consequences. There is no road map on how to handle this type of situation with your child, and sorry seemed hopelessly inadequate. Why God? Why do we keep getting pregnant only to lose our babies? We would get no answers and knew that the pain would only get worse when the actual miscarriage began.

***

The Lord promises to bring peace that passes all understanding through the Holy Spirit. There was no greater time than this for that to be true for our family. We didn't understand, we couldn't imagine this being part of His plan for a greater good. How could the loss of a child be for anything good? Though we were confused and angry at times, without God holding us up while we mourned, surely we would have crumbled.

God blesses those who mourn, for they will be comforted (Matthew 5:4).

CHAPTER 19

THE SHOCK

THURSDAY, JUNE 30th 2016, THE HOSPITAL

Dave and I returned to the hospital Thursday morning to my mom's smiling face. She looked so good it was amazing. Dave brought her some of her things the night before, so she had her makeup, hair brush, and contact lenses to help her feel a little more like herself. The night had passed smoothly, and she got much better sleep being away from the constant noises of the ICU. Breakfast that morning was the first meal she could eat. She had more energy from it, which was great to see. Toward lunch time, Mimi and Justin arrived, and we were all just sitting around talking when her cardiologist from Tuesday morning walked in to see her. Her mouth almost dropped to the floor when she saw my mom.

"I can't believe it!" she exclaimed. "The way you were when you came in Tuesday and how you look now, just sitting up and chatting with everyone, it is miraculous."

It was supposed to be the doctor's one day off that week when she got the page to get to the hospital ASAP at 6:20 a.m. She went on to describe how difficult that morning was, and how she really didn't know if Mom was going to make it. It looked so grim.

"I was trying everything to keep you alive, but I just couldn't figure it out," she confessed.

She even looked to Dave for help at one point and pulled him aside in the hallway to ask some questions, trying to find out any information that might help her with a diagnosis. She asked him if Mom had been stressed lately, because sometimes stress can lead to what's called a "false heart attack." Dave explained that she was diagnosed with breast cancer the day before, but that she really didn't seem overly worried about it. She already had a plan to fight it naturally. He didn't elaborate on exactly what the plan entailed.

Before she had an actual diagnosis, the cardiologist transferred Mom to the care of the ICU doctors and went home for the day. She never knew the full story of Mom's recovery, which is why she was so amazed. By the time the doctor got home around noon on Tuesday, she was already late for a playdate she set up for her five-year-old son. When she arrived, the other mother, whose name was Lindsay, was already at her house waiting.

"I'm so sorry I'm late," she said. "I got called in to an emergency cardiac patient this morning and it was so touch and go."

"Really?" Lindsay asked. "My mother-in-law was taken to the hospital this morning also."

"What is her name?" the cardiologist asked.

"Connie," Lindsay replied.

"Oh my goodness, that was *her*."

Well, as if that day wasn't amazing enough with the way things unfolded, now my brother's wife (Lindsay) took their youngest son to his very first playdate. It was with the son of the cardiologist who just helped to save our mother's life. Lindsay relayed the story to us when she visited that first day, and we were truly astonished.

Although the cardiologist was so happy to see how well Mom was doing, she got serious with her quickly as she approached the bed.

"What is this I hear about you treating your cancer naturally? Cancer is not natural and you have to treat it unnaturally. Surgery is the way to do that. You cannot use nutrition," she told her in a very stern tone.

My mom looked at me shell shocked. First, she had forgotten she had cancer, and none of us brought it up so far. So, the blow of the news hit her so differently than the original diagnosis. The first time she was prepared for it. This time, however, it seemed to hit her out of left field. She looked heartbroken.

As she stared at me for help I assured her, "It's okay Mom, just hear her out."

She trusted in my words and looked back to the doctor to let her finish, but I knew she was confused. I hated seeing her look helpless just when she was beginning to sit up so strong and tall again. The cardiologist continued by saying her brother had cancer, and she believed in supplementing with nutrition but not as a standalone treatment. She recommended Mom have the surgery and radiation and to do it as soon as she was healthy enough.

We thanked her for her time and as the doctor stepped into the hallway, I caught up with her. Here's how much I believed in the plan we had for my mom. I immediately explained to a cardiologist (someone with training way beyond my understanding) regarding something she didn't have any knowledge about, and I did it with absolute confidence. Many times, I feel we just take a doctor's word for things because we know they went to school for such a long period and know infinitely more than we do. But I've also learned something else recently. In the eight years doctors go to school, they only have a one-hour course in nutrition, so it's not something they have experience with. They just don't know what they don't know. I have always loved to learn, and since being introduced to this nutrition, one that is so different and more powerful than anything else out there, I have done my due diligence to find out everything I could about it. I had done the research, so I knew I could share with the doctor a different perspective on how to fight cancer. And I did.

In the hallway, I told the doctor that in no way was I suggesting to my mom that she just eat a lot of fruits and veggies and hope her cancer went away. I would never trust her health to only that type of plan. I explained to her about how extraordinary these products were, how they were patented, something no other nutritional products out there could claim. I shared with her about the 80-plus studies that had been done on them and the science behind them. I know doctors need science, so I knew what information she was going to need to see to understand. Yes, I had already talked to and learned about hundreds, if not thousands, of people who had already used this nutrition successfully to beat cancer, but even that wasn't enough for me by itself. If I was going to go out on a limb and suggest my mom trust her life with something, there had to be science to back it up, and there was. I told the cardiologist of the clinical trial that was currently going on at a highly-respected clinic using these products because of the amazing results doctors saw. The body can do spectacular things if it's given the proper fuel, and that's what this nutrition was designed to do by balancing out the body. The human immune system does the rest. I gave her information on a government website to do more research.

"Well, that's totally different," she said, "not at all what I thought she was going to do. I definitely would like to learn more."

It was very cool to see how excited she got about it (doctors seem to have an innate desire to learn new things and that was evident in her newly found enthusiasm). It was such an about-face from the position she took only moments earlier on Mom's plan to treat her cancer. I always knew God put this in my life for a reason. Now, not only was it going to change Mom's life, but a cardiologist with a brother living in Germany with cancer was going to know about something he may never have heard of without that terrible summer day.

I would follow up with the cardiologist the next week, after she did her research and read more about it. She agreed there were great things happening with it and all the science made sense to her. She was encouraged it was something her brother could use with no side effects, unlike normal treatments, because this was considered food. We set up a time to talk again and to get the information to her brother. Another life that could be changed for the better by what was originally the worst day of our lives. Only God.

***

How can God possibly use our difficulties for a greater good? I just saw the answer to my own question. The near death experience of my mother is nothing I would wish on anyone, and yet if it changed even one other life, I concede to the power of God's plans, because what if this scenario is flipped someday and our family is on the receiving end of glory through tragedy? As difficult as it was, trust wasn't an option, it was a requirement.

> *And we know that God causes everything to work together for the good of those who love God and are called according to his purpose for them (Romans 8:28).*

CHAPTER 20

THE LOSS

SPRING 2013, MYRTLE BEACH, SC

It was April and Canyon was in the middle of his baseball season. It was his favorite sport, and the gorgeous weather of South Carolina made for some wonderful times at the ballpark. During a game about two weeks after our terrible news, though, I knew the miscarriage was about to begin. The familiar pain started, and it was inevitable. Canyon's team was going out for ice cream after the game, and because I knew what was in store for me, I sent him and Charles off to enjoy their time. There was nothing they could do to help me; it was something I had to endure on my own. I had done it before and would just have to do it again. Charles has always been very supportive emotionally, but he could do nothing to help with the physical part.

About a half hour after I got home, I realized this was going to be different from my other miscarriages. I could only assume it was because I was much further along into my pregnancy than in the past. Charles came home and put Canyon to bed, as I was unable to leave the bathroom for the next thirty minutes. I continued to make numerous trips back to the bathroom for the next few hours and became nauseated from the blood loss. Getting back to the bed became more difficult each time as the room started spinning. At around 3 a.m., I passed out near the sink and Charles had to lift me off the floor. Luckily, I didn't hit anything as I fell, but he had seen enough, and off to the ER we went. These types of situations were even more difficult, because we had to handle everything on our own with no family around. We had to wake up Canyon and take him with us.

After a few hours at the hospital, the doctor gave me lots of fluids and said I was fine to go home. I should just take it easy, and the miscarriage should be over very soon. Charles and I were both relieved. However, as it turned out, the doctor would be wrong. I continued to have problems for two more weeks, so Charles said I had to go back because something just didn't seem normal. He was right. Apparently, I had what was called a "partial miscarriage," and that was why I was continuing to bleed. The thought of it was awful for me. My doctor gave me medicine to help my progress.

The process was hard enough without it continuing for weeks, and it was taking an emotional toll on all of us. We could only hope it would be over soon and we could try to go back to everyday life. But the miscarriage process, which sadly became part of our lives for the fourth time, would soon become a scare we were not expecting. The following weekend we were at a friend's house for a party when suddenly my body quickly took a turn for the worst. I immediately headed for the closest bathroom. There was absolutely no way I could stand, as the blood loss was extreme, so my friend found Charles and Canyon. We decided I had to try to head for the car to go back to the emergency room, and fast.

As Charles guided me to the car, my knees went weak, and he had to keep me steady. As we drove off, Canyon began asking all kinds of questions. As I mentioned earlier, he is very observant and was extremely concerned about me. I started to feel lightheaded and was wracked with pain, but I did my best to let him know everything was fine. We just needed to get to a doctor to have them check on me, and I would feel better soon. I remember Charles also asking me some questions, but the more he talked, the more he seemed to be in a tunnel. Soon I could barely hear him at all. I knew he was saying something, but I wasn't sure what it was.

The next thing I remember was Charles yelling my name, over and over and Canyon crying in the back of the car. Apparently, I passed out and threw up all over myself. Charles was unable to wake me for what

I am sure felt like an eternity to him. He was concerned I was going to choke and was paralyzed, unable to help as he had to continue to drive quickly to the ER. Fortunately, the hospital was only a few more minutes away. Charles ran in to inform the staff what happened, and their reactions let me know this was serious. When I had come here a few weeks ago, we waited for a half hour to see someone, but this time I was immediately rushed to a room. I remember faintly hearing someone say "level 4." From the frantic amount of activity going on around me, I knew "level 4" was reason for concern, but with the pain I was in there was no time to worry.

That was my last memory before waking up the next morning. Charles filled me in on the details of the night. I had emergency surgery, and had lost so much blood that I needed a transfusion. Charles looked like he had been through the ringer, having to juggle what was happening to me and care for Canyon all at the same time. He was undoubtedly scared by how suddenly things went south. It was a frightening night. We never considered that a miscarriage would be a danger to my life. But it took us only a few days to decide that after this experience, we were done. We were not having any more children. God blessed us with Canyon and although we mapped out different plans for the size of our family, we succumbed to what seemed to be obvious. Another child was just not meant to be. We were thankful for the three of us and that God spared my life in our latest tragedy. That was enough.

***

This was, without a doubt, one of the lowest times in our lives. We knew that God had a plan for us, but how were our broken hearts a part of it? We needed God more than ever in the midst of this valley. We had to believe that He wasn't done with us yet.

CHAPTER 21

THE TRANSFER

FRIDAY, JULY 1st 2016, THE HOSPITAL

The doctor informed us Thursday night that if everything looked good in the morning, he would send Mom to a bigger hospital for the defibrillator procedure. When Dave and I arrived Friday morning, the plans were already set in motion, and she was to be transferred around noon. It felt great knowing we were going to leave this place behind. Although she made an amazing recovery, I was happy to say goodbye to the scary memories that still haunted me each time I pulled into the parking lot.

The paramedics arrived to get Mom ready, and it was the same crew that worked on her Tuesday morning. Small world. Even more amazing was the fact that one of them was the woman who bought my childhood home from Charles and me ten years prior. She was a critical part of keeping my mom alive that morning—just one more incredible piece of the story. They all marveled at how well she was doing and told her how they were amazed she made it. Loading her into the ambulance this day was a much happier time, as I watched my mom talk with them and smile as they wheeled her out the door. We had one more hurdle to jump, and that was a successful procedure to protect her heart.

As I drove the half hour to the next hospital, I thought back on the last few days. The number of miracles God performed, both large and small, were enough to make me weep.

God breathed new life into my mom and kept our family strong during this time of chaos. His glory was surrounding us everywhere we looked, and we knew He held all of us in His arms.

God brought Mom back from the dead and released me from a potential lifetime of guilt for not calling her back Monday night. He placed numerous people exactly where they needed to be at the exact moments they needed to be there. He answered the prayers for healing, and showed us that He was in control and always would be. It was a glorious week, and although it was not over yet I could not deny His presence every step of the way. Mom still had one procedure left to endure, and I was confident she would be okay. I knew enough by now to place these circumstances in greater hands and stand back to watch Him work.

The rest of Friday afternoon was spent prepping Mom for the defibrillator procedure and answering any questions the medical staff had about what transpired that week. The only recent change was that instead of her blood pressure being low, it was now extremely high. It was a concern to the family, but the doctors didn't seem to question it at all, so we were again left to trust in the process. By this point, Dave also brought her nutritional supplements to the hospital, because if she was able to eat, she could take them. I felt better about her body getting what it needed to be strong. There were so many powerful drugs with potential side effects put in her body trying to keep her alive that we knew she needed as much good as we could get in her at this point. She certainly didn't have a big appetite and wasn't taking much in, but anything was better than nothing.

The procedure was supposed to take a little over an hour, and at the two-hour mark I began to feel nervous but just continued to wait in her room. I knew she had to be coming any time now. A few minutes later, she was wheeled in. She was groggy and slightly disoriented, but everything had gone perfectly. You could see exactly where they inserted the defibrillator on her left side, and it would always be a reminder of that day. But for the first time all week, we knew she had what was necessary to keep her safe for the future. Three days ago, it was a future we weren't sure she was going to have. The doctor told us he noticed her extra beats during the surgery. That was frightening to hear, but hopefully lightning would never strike twice for her.

That afternoon my older brother Ryan called Mom, and she beamed at hearing his voice. I listened to her relay what details she could now remember about dying and tell of her disappointment at not meeting Jesus. My mom has read every book ever written about people dying and going to Heaven, and now that she had died she really wished she could have had the same experience.

She asked him incredulously, "Can you believe I didn't get to meet Jesus!"

I am sure Ryan was smiling on the other end of the phone, amused that this was the scenario Mom was thinking about at this point in her recovery. But I know he was just grateful she was alive and doing so well. As they ended the call, I could see talking to Ryan gave Mom an extra boost to her spirit. It always did.

Later that night Dave's mom and dad visited, and it was amazing to see his dad in perfect health after his stroke Tuesday morning. If you didn't know his story, you would not believe it happened, looking at him in person. The family visited with Mom into the early evening and reminisced on the week. She still couldn't remember all the details of that morning, but each day brought a little more retention, so we weren't as worried about her brain long term. She just was going to need time, and having time was something to cherish after all that she had been through. Her cardiologist explained to us her belief that not remembering such a tragic event was the brain's way of protecting itself from the harsh reality of the event. I'm sure if you asked Dave, knowing all the details firsthand is something he wished he didn't have so deeply rooted into his brain. Those details formed a chronicle he would never forget, even if he tried.

***

If you had told me that three days after my mom died that she would be healthy enough to be transferred to a regular hospital room, I would have never believed it. Our human eyes cannot see the supernatural and what is working around us through Jesus and His healing powers. She was meant to rise.

> *Stretch out your hand with healing power; may miraculous signs and wonders be done through the name of your holy servant Jesus (Acts 4:30).*

CHAPTER 22

THE CURVE

SUMMER 2013, MYRTLE BEACH, SC

As the end of summer approached and my health improved, I began thinking about going back to work, as Canyon would be in school from the beginning of first grade. My teaching certification lapsed from being out of the profession for so long, so I starting thinking about other things. With all the moves we made and the constant search for new homes to live in, I became intrigued by real estate. I loved seeing the inside of new houses and imagining their possibilities. I knew how much a good fit meant to us, and wanted to help find that for other people.

For the next few weeks, I went to real estate school every day, all day. It was intense and I had much to learn. But just as Canyon started school that fall, I received my license and found a job with a company in town. It was exciting, and I was happy to find something positive to focus on after the difficult summer we just experienced.

As the first few months of the school year went by, I worked part time so I could be very involved with Canyon at school. I dropped him off and picked him up each day and ate lunch with him once a week. I also went on all the field trips. (One of them was to the local bowling alley; I never quite figured out what was educational about that trip.)

A few times a week, I took educational classes for my new job on some of the finer points of real estate. Even after you get your license, the number of things to know never seemed to end. In real life, it was nothing like real estate "reality shows" you see on TV. There were a lot of behind-the-scenes details that were not much fun, which, I am sure, is why they don't show them.

In one of my classes, they were teaching us how to get referrals. This was going to be key for me, as I only knew a handful of people. They all already had homes and did not need an agent. I was going to have to actively seek people who could send their friends my way. It was a very new concept to me as I am outgoing when I get to know someone, but not as much right away.

On one of Canyon's field trips, I connected with a couple I had noticed many times visiting the school during lunch and attending classroom parties. On more than one occasion, I wondered what they did. It is very unusual to see both parents at every school function, but it was the two of them all the time. Charles rarely got to come to anything because one us had to be working, and it was him. The couple's names were Norm and Sheila, and they were extremely friendly. They always had smiles on their faces and said hello. Many times after I walked Canyon into the school in the morning, I would see them praying with their daughter in the car. I thought that was cool, and they would be great people to get to know.

Because of Sheila's friendly appearance, I made her my first attempt at getting referrals and used my newfound knowledge to get my business off the ground. I was going to smoothly work my way over to her and strike up a conversation. I knew she would make it easy for me, because I could tell she was very outgoing. I introduced myself, and we made small talk about seeing each other around and which one was our child. After a few minutes, I casually let her know what I did for a living and asked if she had any real estate needs. She didn't. Oh-for-one. But, she said she'd let her friends know about me just in case. That's all I could ask for, so I was pleased with how the conversation went. As I was about to turn away, *she* casually mentioned that sometime I should hear more about what she and her husband did.

"Uh, sure," I responded as she handed me her card. I had no intention of looking at anything, but wasn't going to be rude as she had been nothing but kind to me.

I found the card later that week when I was doing the laundry, and I had some extra time that day. I decided, *why not just take a peek?* I went to her website and saw she worked as an independent distributor for a nutrition company. Well, that explained it; she worked for herself and made her own hours. I scanned the information and thought it looked good, but I really had no experience with nutritional supplements, so I wasn't exactly sure what I was looking at. I stayed home with Canyon from the beginning, so I just did my best to feed him as healthily as I could. I thought I was doing well, even though he still got sick quite often. So, I didn't really need any of what she was selling. But good for her and her husband, if that's how they were supporting their family and still had the time to be at their daughter's important school functions.

I really thought that would be where our paths would end. I would see Sheila and Norm around school for the next few months and give a wave in passing. A few times, Sheila would tell me we really should get together for lunch so she could tell me more, because the supplements were truly changing people's lives, both with their health and their incomes. Because she was so nice, I just continued to say "Sure," but never had any thoughts of following through. I was intrigued by how she could support her family doing this job, but when I start something new I give it my all. I wanted to become successful at real estate and didn't want to be distracted. I also had that natural skepticism that kept me from believing that what she said could be true.

Fast forward six months, and I was at a restaurant, sitting down to lunch with Sheila. I was doing exactly what I told Charles many times I would never do. Why did I change my mind? Well, once again God detoured *my* plans and threw our family a curveball I would have never imagined in my wildest dreams.

And so, I agreed to lunch. "Don't worry," I assured Charles. "I have no plans of doing anything. I'm just going to listen and get something to eat." It would be the greatest promise I have ever broken.

You can make many plans, but the Lord's purpose will prevail (Proverbs 19:21).

CHAPTER 23

THE RELEASE

SATURDAY, JULY 2nd 2016, THE HOSPITAL

Four days after having forty-five minutes of life saving CPR performed, Mom was going home. The funny part was, between Dave, Justin, and me, none of us were looking at that as a good thing. Her blood pressure was still extremely high, and even though the doctors tried different medications, it wasn't coming down much. We wanted her to stay another night to be monitored, but they said it wasn't worth the risk of her contracting some sort of infection from being around all the germs in the hospital. Her numbers were acceptable in their eyes. Doctors, of course, are the ones with all the experience and knew it was unnecessary, so we allowed ourselves to be happy about her release. I mean, really, we should have been celebrating this momentous occasion. I don't know what a normal recovery time is from what she went through, but going home within four days seemed impossible. Then I remembered that doctors from the ICU at the first hospital had told us she would be in the hospital at least a week. A phenomenal recovery? Absolutely. But at this point, it seemed to align with the rest of the week by destroying the odds and defying what seemed logical medically.

Mom was all smiles about going home. She was her bright and bubbly self as we gathered up her things and thanked all the staff for helping her get to this point. She was as gracious as it gets. We were ready to take our last trip down the elevators, with Mom in tow for the first time. She was excited to sleep in her own home, rest on her own couch, and be surrounded by those she loved. For the rest of us, it would be the first opportunity to see her in a setting outside the hospital for the first time in a week, and try to forget the difficult memories as we moved forward.

As we got Mom settled into the living room of her house, we talked about the week again and the amazing journey she had traveled. We went through the entire story from the beginning as she still couldn't retain the whole thing.

"I'm going to have to make you some sort of journal," I told her, "because I don't know if you're ever going to be able to fully remember, and you really need to see how many miracles were performed this week."

She agreed and looked forward to having it written down so she could go back through the experience. As she shifted to get more comfortable, she winced in pain. This would be the first time any of us would see the results from the defibrillator paddles on her chest. As she looked down, it was obvious what caused her so much discomfort. She had a red burn, an inch wide and about three inches long, running down her chest. Her mouth dropped open, and she looked confused about what she was seeing.

"That's from how many times they shocked you. It was seven times in all, we think," Dave explained.

I can't imagine what it's like to really take in that type of information, but as I watched my mom gently rub the burn, it was evident it was overwhelming and incomprehensible. We have watched doctor shows together many times throughout the years, and I believe she was thinking what I had thought—nobody comes back when they shock you that many times. And if they do, they are never the same. But here we sat together, looking at a perfectly healthy woman, aside from the scars from her defibrillator surgery and paddle burns. She was talking and smiling and going about her night, enjoying her family when she really shouldn't be here at all. The scars would be the greatest reminders of a day in our family's history when God reached down from heaven and touched Mom's body with His hands. He did what no medical doctor could have done—brought her back from the depths of darkness.

At a follow-up appointment with her cardiologist weeks later, the doctor confirmed what we already knew, but it was amazing coming from a scientific viewpoint.

"I was doing everything I could to save you, but I was failing," the doctor explained. "Sometimes we do everything right and the patient dies. Sometimes we don't have any idea what to do and the patient lives. That was you and that is only explained by God."

Amen.

Mom spent the rest of the afternoon dozing occasionally. The day was great but exhausting for her. As the light of day began to fade, she wanted to go outside and see her pond. She and Dave had stocked it with koi the year before, and watching those fish brought her a lot of joy. As she stood outside with Dave, I got a text from my brother telling me he was almost there. A smile crept across my face, because I knew this day was about to get exponentially better for my mom. It wasn't my brother Justin who sent me that text. It was Ryan, the brother who lived in Las Vegas, the brother we only got to see every few years. Until I had my own children, I could never really understand what Mom meant when she talked of how her heart physically hurt when she couldn't see her children. Ryan was the one she saw the least, and it was painful for her. He lived across the country, so it wasn't an easy trip to make. Since having my own boys, I could begin to empathize. I couldn't imagine going a year or two without seeing them. But she wasn't going to have to miss Ryan much longer, as Dave had secretly been talking to him throughout the week. They arranged for Ryan and his wife Cassandra to fly in as a special gift for Mom.

After they arrived, Ryan and Cassandra crept around the side of the house to surprise Mom. As she turned around to walk back in the door, she saw them and was flooded with euphoria. If she was able to run, she would have, I'm sure. But instead she threw her arms open wide, encouraging him to come to her and beamed with pleasure. I always felt that she could hold on to him for hours, given the opportunity, but she eventually let him go, and we went inside. He told her he could stay four days, and she was thrilled. Having Ryan and his wife at her side was just what she needed, and they would be so helpful, not just physically but emotionally. It was especially comforting for me, because Charles had already taken off work since Tuesday, and I had to go home to take care of the kids. I really didn't want Mom to be alone because Dave also had to return to his job on Monday. It was working out just perfectly and was such an important lift for Mom. She has always put on a brave face through obstacles, but I knew there would be times coming up that the weight of what happened would come crashing down on her. But for now, she could still be distracted by having all her children with her at one time.

***

Love. There is nothing greater—the love of a mother, the love of a child, and ultimately the love of Jesus. It trumps all sadness, all despair, and all sense of hopelessness. God was great and His love for my mother was radiating from her. She was wrapped in His love, and I could go home knowing His arms would continue to hold her close.

Three things will last forever—faith, hope, and love—and the greatest of these is love (1 Corinthians 13:13).

CHAPTER 24

THE DETOUR

JANUARY 2014, MYRTLE BEACH, SC

Our family spent Christmas in Pennsylvania as usual, and as we were traveling the twelve hours back to Myrtle Beach, I started to feel sick. It wasn't a big deal; I was just not my normal self. I always caught at least one winter cold along with a flu or two, so I didn't think much of it. I planned to focus on real estate after the holiday and was excited to get going. The only problem was, when Monday came I was not any better. In fact, I was worse and unable to get out of bed. Charles and I assumed it was the flu, but as the week drug on I became frustrated because there were things I wanted to do, and I just wasn't able.

By Friday Charles asked, "You don't think you could be pregnant, do you?"

That was the very last thing I wanted to be happening. I knew it was almost impossible, because I started paying more attention, so we had no more surprises like the last time. But as the day progressed, I decided to find out for sure because it was starting to nag at me. I decided to have Charles bring me a test just to confirm I wasn't pregnant. Then, I figured I would just have to suck it up and push through this sickness—use the power of positive thinking to stop letting it drag on.

It took me about an hour to get up the nerve to take the test, and I will never forget how quickly the positive sign showed up. Unbelievable. I immediately called Charles, sobbing, and relayed the news.

"Is this a happy cry?" he asked.

In years past, we both got weepy at the blessing of a pregnancy, but this time it was not the case.

"*Noooo!*" I wailed. "These pregnancies don't work out for us, and I don't want to go through this again!"

After years of praying to have another child, I had changed my prayer recently and begged God not to ever let me get pregnant again, because I could not endure another miscarriage. This was not what I wanted, not at all.

***

A few months later, I was sitting at a table having lunch with Sheila. She finally caught up with me in the school hallway one day, and I told her one of the reasons I hadn't gotten back to her (she had called me a few times) was that I was expecting and not feeling well.

I remember her smiling so big, and me instantly saying, "No, we don't get excited. Pregnancies don't end well for us, so we are not happy."

I could tell those words shocked her because she was naturally a positive person, and normally so was I. It was a difficult thing to say, but it was how I felt.

Sheila gave me my space for the next three months and would just have people who were involved in the same company with her leave messages on my phone, telling me the amazing health results they got with the products, along with financial success. They spoke of the way the products and the business drastically changed their lives. I thought the health results were great, but it was the business that intrigued me in the beginning. Now that I was close to six months pregnant, there seemed to be a glimmer of hope we would get to meet the baby. I was so sure we would lose this one too that I didn't even tell my mom until I was close to five months pregnant.

I knew working in real estate would be impossible with a newborn, and after listening to so many stories about people working their own schedule and having a lifestyle they always dreamed about, I was up for hearing more about Sheila's company. To be able to build an income based on helping other people was starting to sound like the perfect job.

After our lunch date, I was bubbling with excitement. Now I really started to understand what these nutritional supplements were all about and how they were so different from anything else on the market. The next month I went to a meeting with about twenty other people and got to hear firsthand how lives were changed. People shared stories about heart surgeries that were scheduled but never happened, about how one woman's body was so broken she should be paralyzed but was now running marathons. It was beyond moving and watching the passion people had was amazing. There were so many different inspirational testimonies I could no longer deny this was real. I learned this was the best of both worlds. I could change people's lives with their health and change our own lives by working around my baby and eventually making enough income that Charles could retire because of the business potential. I was in. And that's when the light bulb turned on. The first person I knew needed to hear about this was my mom.

Remember the neck pain that forced her into early retirement? Well, it had been eighteen years since the day it started, and I had prayed without ceasing for a miracle, but nothing ever changed. She struggled through each day the best she could, and lying down every few hours just became a normal routine. We all knew not to schedule a full day of activities without including time for breaks to rest her neck. We also could not take her on bumpy roads. We didn't want to do anything that would make her pain worse. And every six months, the doctor checked her kidneys because of the side effects of long-term narcotic use. Year after year, there were never any new ideas on how to help her. At 48, she had been condemned to live a life in pain—end of story.

Except now I saw *hope*. I heard stories of people just like her who were now pain free, and I wanted nothing more than for her to be one of them. I had to share this with her!

It's funny how we see certain events in our lives as detours when they were plans God had all along. We just weren't given the schedule in advance. All those years we could never quite understand our journey.

We embraced it as best we could and made the best of it, but there were easier paths we could have taken. And given *our* way, Myrtle Beach would not have been where we chose to be at this point of our lives.

Why did we have to move to eight different states? Why didn't some of Charles's jobs work out the way we had planned or the way we were promised? Why did we have to drag our child all over the country, never allowing him a chance to make lasting friendships? Why did we feel the nudge to go to South Carolina instead of Las Vegas? Why did I finally have a healthy baby after four miscarriages—a baby who became the sole reason I finally looked at this opportunity? If I hadn't become pregnant, I wouldn't have given this a second thought. I would have continued with real estate, no question. And how did we finally find an answer to years of silent suffering and pain for the woman who means everything to me?

God, that's how. We are not in control and if we do our best to live by God's will, then He takes care of all the details in His own timing.

***

This part of our lives gives me a vision of when someone takes your hand, puts a blindfold on your eyes and says, "Just trust me," as they lead you through an obstacle course. I know I so badly want to reach out to keep myself from running into something, and I almost lean backward to ward off the pain of hitting something hard. But if it was some type of competition, the team that would win would be the one with the blindfolded partner willing to hold nothing back and forge full speed ahead, having full confidence in their leader. I can't say I have always had the strength to go full speed ahead. I have been weak many times, but I am thankful we never gave up on doing our best to follow our leader.

> *Jesus spoke to the people once more and said, "I am the light of the world. If you follow me, you won't have to walk in darkness, because you will have the light that leads to life"* (John 8:12).

CHAPTER 25

THE GUILT

SUNDAY, JULY 3rd 2016, MOM'S HOUSE, PA

I didn't give my mom much time to celebrate her homecoming. This had been the hardest week of all our lives, and Mom's journey back to health was unquestionably miraculous. She returned from the depths of despair and came out victorious. The family was so grateful for the work God did to save her. It would have been wonderful to just soak in the moment and relish her being out of the hospital. However, she still had cancer. Her next fight for life needed to begin, and it needed to start right away in my opinion. By the next morning, we already talked about her cancer and her plan to fight it with the nutritional products. I was more than ready to get her started, because I hated the thought of cancer being in her body. I wanted to embark on the healing process as soon as she felt able.

Here's what you need to know about this nutrition—the reasons I was willing to trust it with my mom's life and be the person who suggested the plan. If it didn't work, I knew my relationship with my family would never be the same, and there would be no way I could blame anyone for how they would feel about me. But, I never once had a second thought about it, because this wasn't like anything else out on the market. There were years and years' worth of clinical studies done on a game-changing ingredient the products had that no other company in the world possessed. This company had the patent on it. It is the first nutrition to ever get such an honor, and they didn't have just one patent in their arsenal, they had ten. Getting a patent on something considered food is nearly impossible, but they did it. That meant they had to prove these ingredients were unique. I also met the president of the company and saw his heart to help people. I spoke with the scientists who discovered and worked on this nutrition for almost thirty years. I was fully confident in what I had suggested.

Many clinical trials were performed with these products because of what they had done for people. Doctors took notice and asked for the products as word of their success spread. The patented ingredient had been shown to do so many things; two of its unique effects were its ability to encapsulate cancer, as well as suppress tumors with *no side effects*. The company never promised a cure, but the human immune system can do amazing things given the proper fuel, and that's what it was doing with a multitude of diseases time and time again.

That's where Mom and I were totally on the same page. We respected anyone's choice for their personal treatment, especially those who didn't know anything about these products. I knew of hundreds of people who used these supplements along with their treatment, which helped their protocol to work better. It also kept side effects at bay by building their body's healthy cells when treatment destroyed them. But I also knew so many who used them as their only treatment, and that's what my mom decided to do. She didn't want surgery, radiation, or chemotherapy. I made it very clear to her that I believed if God was going to take you, He was going to take you, because that is my faith. But from what the science showed, if we put enough product in her body and gave it ample time, I knew she would be cancer free eventually. So, the plan was set in motion.

The last few days in the hospital she took only one or two shakes a day because it was all she could do, but I was chomping at the bit to really get her going and start flooding her body with the products. She wanted to stick to the original plan and decided to go *"all in"* from that day forward. My mom always told me she had issues with certain tastes and was sensitive to new flavors, but we were going to put everything she needed all in one shake from the very start, and it was a lot. I knew it was going to take some time for her to get used to. She had been taking her shakes with chocolate milk to make them taste better, but now that she had cancer this was no longer an option. Research shows cancer feeds on sugar, and to give herself the best chance she had to cut it out, and she agreed to do it.

So, the first Sunday back from the hospital we put the plan in motion. I went to the kitchen and got her first shake ready. These shakes were made from a powder. It was important, once they were activated with water, to drink them within twenty minutes to get the most potency out of them. She was going to take six of them a day, so she needed to get moving and drink them quickly. She promised to do her best, and I knew she would. We were putting multiple ingredients in her shake, and a few were new to her, so I knew the taste was going to be an adjustment. But I was ill-prepared for what was to come. Here's where I wish I would have thought this through a bit more. She had just had the worst week of her life, and her body had been pumped with a multitude of nasty drugs. Her system was completely out of whack. The problem with your body being in that state is that it affects your taste buds even more than normal. I should have suggested she work her way up, but I didn't. I admittedly had tunnel vision, and I would sorely regret that choice.

I handed her the shake. She was going to take large gulps and down it as fast as she could. Her first gulp, and she was starting to dry heave. Oh my goodness, what was I thinking? She immediately got off the couch and headed hastily for the bathroom with Dave by her side to keep her steady. She hadn't really moved that quickly in a week, but she felt as though she was going to throw up. For the next few minutes, I heard her gagging and crying simultaneously. With each gag, she was causing herself more and more pain in her chest, where they had performed compressions to keep her alive. We didn't even know she was that sore until that time, but now it was evident. She is a tough lady, but was clearly in severe pain.

It was the longest five minutes of my life as the guilt overwhelmed me. I felt personally responsible for her suffering, and there was nothing I wanted more than to take it away for her, but I was helpless. I prayed fervently for it to end as soon as possible.

When it was over, she walked out of the bathroom with tears streaming down her face, looked at me and said, "I'm sorry, I'll do better next time."

She was sorry? She had nothing to feel badly about; I did. But she didn't blame me for a second, and that attitude was exactly where I received my strength throughout my life. She was a warrior and was going to do this—but not today.

Her body was just not ready yet, and as she got settled back on the couch, we made some modifications for the coming week. We would ease her into the process and give her body some time to adjust to the taste by tweaking a few things. The week's trauma had her starting at a deficit because her taste buds had really been affected by all the medications that had been put into her.

In only two days, her body made huge strides to get balanced, and by day three she had no problem with the taste. I must admit I thanked God multiple times, because on that first day I really questioned whether she would be able to go this route. If her body was going to react that way to every shake, she was never going to get six in each day. But again, God provided a way, and after some bumps in the beginning she picked up speed and by week two was at full throttle and doing a great job. She was going to kick that cancer out of her body. I had no doubt.

The Lord is for me, so I will have no fear. What can mere people do to me? (Psalms 118:6)

CHAPTER 26

THE ANSWER

AUGUST 2014, MYRTLE BEACH, SC

The best of intentions get sidetracked sometimes. Even though I planned to work with this company and share the hope of the products with my mom and others, it was late summer and I was very pregnant and distracted by my discomfort. Every week I told myself I would get going, but I continued to push it back as I was having a miserable final trimester. I couldn't sleep because of carpal tunnel in my arms, and the South Carolina heat was wreaking havoc on my body. So, starting a business was on the back burner for the moment, with plans to get to it as soon as I could.

We were just so blown away by the fact that this baby was healthy and we were going to meet him soon. It was difficult to think of much else. We knew he was a miracle. It didn't seem real, except when I looked down at my ever-growing belly. Canyon went with us to our six-month ultrasound to find out the sex and I will never forget his look of pure joy when we found out it was a boy. He was so certain it was a girl and still excited, but at the words "it's a boy," he instantly beamed. It was unforgettable.

Near the end of the summer, we welcomed our second son Maverick, more than five years from when we first tried for another child. What a roller coaster of joy and pain we experienced in that time. We lost four babies in three different states and moved six times. Life took us closer to family, only to then be ripped back apart. Promising career paths for Charles—opportunities we thought were leading us back home again—

never worked out. I found a career in real estate I thought would be part of our history of moving. It wasn't. But God protected this child and gave him to us, even though doctors said it would be unlikely to ever happen without medical intervention. And he wasn't just any baby; he was a 10 pound 2 ounce whopper! I will never forget the words of the anesthesiologist when he came out.

"Congratulations, you have a baby toddler!" he declared.

It was awesome and just so perfect. He was as healthy as could be and made a big entrance into our world, just as he was meant to do. Sheila and her husband Norm were two of only a handful of people who visited us in the hospital, and it meant a lot. With no family around to celebrate with us, it was very cool to share in the joy with them. We had become a lot closer over the last few months and enjoyed sharing family time together. After my first few weeks at home, Sheila called to see if she could visit.

"Absolutely!" I said, as I was going a little stir crazy like all new mothers. Canyon was in school, Charles was at work, and I had no one to talk to.

She didn't mention the nutritional products or the business once during her visit. But I did. I started feeling selfish about keeping the information to myself, when it could be helping others, especially my mom. When Maverick was six weeks old, I called my mom. I told her I found the answer to her pain. I will never forget Sheila asking her when she thought she'd like to get started.

My mom answered, "Well, today, of course!"

Mom would tell me months later she didn't really have any expectations about the products, but just trusted me. I could never put into words how that level of trust feels. She knew I thought about her pain constantly, even though I couldn't feel it. I researched for years to see if there was anything that could help her, but there didn't seem to be. I think we both just accepted there was no solution to her problem, but thankfully we were mistaken and in a big way.

Six months after starting on the products, my mom took her very last narcotic and her neck no longer hurt. She was free from the chains of chronic pain. I explained how important it was to be consistent day in and day out for this to work because nutrition is different. It was designed to heal her body from the inside out and help it become balanced. She followed every bit of advice and the products delivered. As I write this today, she has been symptom free for eighteen months, and it has been life-changing. She got off the anti-depressants she was prescribed so many years previously because she no longer deals with everyday pain. She also doesn't have the numerous side effects associated with the narcotics she was taking anymore.

To this day, it's easy to forget how great she feels, because during a very busy day sometimes one of us will ask her if she needs to rest.

She always looks at us like we're crazy and responds, "Why would I have to do that?"

For us, it is just years of conditioning from what we remember her life to be. But now she is a new woman and can enjoy life at a whole new level. It's remarkable. She wants no part of looking back to what was, only to enjoy each day to the fullest and look forward to the times to come.

We now have two new babies—Maverick, and my brother Justin's fourth child—whom she can savor her time with in a way we never thought possible. In most of my pictures taken when Canyon was young, my mom is lying down. It's just how it was. But now, she babysits my brother's daughter a few days a week. It's unbelievable when I think back to what her pain level has been over the last eighteen years. She's 68 years old now and taking care of a two-year-old by herself with absolute ease. Her sixties are more enjoyable than her forties were.

Of course, I wish I would've known about this so many years ago when my mom first starting having the pain. It made life so difficult for her. She retired before she was ready and just couldn't enjoy the things she used to love. She had to constantly "fake" her way through each day. She continuously stretched her neck around just trying to find a comfortable position that would ease the pain, but she never found relief. Every day when she woke up, she knew the pain would be there waiting.

But now I couldn't be more grateful to Sheila, a total stranger God placed in my life at just the right time for just the right reason. We have been working together ever since that call to my mom one October night in 2014. And more than two years later, it is so much more than a business relationship. Sheila has become part of our family and one of my very best friends. Maverick calls her Aunty She-She. She visited him every week since he was six weeks old until the day we left South Carolina, when he was eleven months old. Our families have been on vacation together. We talk several times a week and always will. And my mom's life would never have been so radically changed without God nudging me to approach Sheila on that field trip. Was it about real estate referrals? Not even close. This was an answer to prayer after eighteen years. God did not forsake His child to live a life of pain. He was just not done weaving His perfect plan together and using His timing. We were so grateful for this blessing. And this was all before we'd find out Mom had cancer fifteen months later and that it had been growing in her body for close to nine years.

***

I know there were times when my mom felt like she was imprisoned by her pain. But God broke her chains and set her free. He made a way when there didn't seem to be one.

> *God is our refuge and strength, always ready to help in times of trouble (Psalms 46:1).*

CHAPTER 27

THE WAIT

SEPTEMBER 2016, PENNSYLVANIA

My mom had been on the nutritional products for a little over two months by this point, and I had to give her credit. Her schedule was not easy to keep. She was taking a shake every two and a half hours and having to plan her day around them anytime she wanted to go somewhere. She also made big changes to her diet, completely cutting out sugar and eating almost exclusively fruits and vegetables to give her body the best chance to be healthy again.

It was about this time, though, that she was starting to falter just a little and called me. She was being honest about having trouble getting that sixth shake in, and unbeknownst to me had been skipping it for a few weeks. She said she couldn't figure out a way to fit it in. This was certainly not something I wanted to hear, because I wanted her body to have everything it needed to heal itself. I felt every shake was crucial to help the process. I heard lots of stories of people being healed with these products who were taking a lot less than she was. But as I told her from the start, those people were not *my* mother. I wanted to treat her cancer like it was stage 4—you have two weeks to live and want to get it out of there as quickly as possible. More product was the way to do that.

The difficult part about this situation for me was that I was smack dab in the crosshairs of it all. I was the middle-man to explain everything to family members and friends about the products and the details regarding each shake. I also explained the foods she was eating and why she was eating them. In addition, I felt like Mom's conscience, telling her what to eat because she always looked to me for her selections. I didn't like being in a position to treat her like a child by telling her what to do. I wanted to be there for her every step of the way, so I was still glad she turned to me. And I would do it again in a heartbeat, but it didn't mean that it was ideal.

It's not like I didn't understand why it was this way, because the details of her plan came from my suggestions. I had put myself in this situation, but even I didn't always feel like I had an answer to every question possible. I am not a nutritionist, but I did research what foods were best for her. I knew the ins and outs of the products, but didn't know how to get her to take all her shakes. It was sometimes overwhelming, but I wasn't going to feel sorry for myself. My mom was the one with cancer, and she was fighting, so I would continue to support her the very best way I could. She was still human, though, and changing your life in an instant is hard to do for months at a time. I did my best to empathize.

Even though this schedule was difficult to maintain, we were still grateful Mom wasn't going through radiation or chemotherapy, which would have been much more intense, and would have had definite side effects. I give all the credit in the world to people who endure that treatment, because I can't pretend to relate to how grueling it must be.

I had no answers to help my mom during that call, so I did the only thing I knew how to do that night and prayed about it. By morning, I had an idea. I felt good about it, but it's so hard to know how Mom would react, so I was slightly worried. I spent about an hour putting my thoughts on paper and mailed it out to her that day. I crossed my fingers and prayed it would be encouraging in the way she needed it to be.

Three days later I got a text from my mom that read, "Well, you really know how to motivate someone!"

Thank goodness. I could breathe a sigh of relief. What was my idea? It looked a little like this:

SUCCESS SCHEDULE

7:00 am for NOAH

9:30 am for CANYON

12 pm for GABRIEL

2:30 pm for MASON

5:00 pm for MAVERICK

7:30 pm for LEAH FAITH

Those were the names of her six grandchildren—one name for each of the six shakes she needed to take daily. I knew I was taking a chance of being passive-aggressive with the schedule, but it ended up having the desired effect. She wasn't offended at all.

When I would check in with her a week later to see how the schedule was working and if she was getting all her shakes in she said, "Of course I am. How could I ever skip my Leah Faith?"

My mom never missed that sixth shake again. And how poetic that her last grandchild was the only one in the family with a middle name like Faith, a perfect motivator. I smiled the next time I came to her house and saw the schedule up on the refrigerator as a daily reminder.

Anytime I would come over after that she would say things to me like, "I've already taken Mason; let's go," or "Just a minute, I need to take Maverick before we leave."

It was adorable. I knew she was headed for success; now all we had to do was wait for it.

***

There have been so many times in my life I've worried. I've worried about jobs, finances, parenting, and many others things for sure. Though God tells us to cast our cares on Him, I admit I have been weak. But I can honestly say I was never truly worried about my mom's cancer. I felt so certain God put the nutrition in my path for this time because He knew Mom already had cancer in her body and was going to need it. I was at peace as we waited for God to move.

As for me, I look to the Lord for help. I wait confidently for God to save me, and my God will certainly hear me (Micah 7:7).

CHAPTER 28

THE SALE

MAY 2015, MYRTLE BEACH, SC

L ife was good. We had a new baby, Mom was out of pain, and I was busy helping others by sharing with them about the hope for good health with the products. Canyon liked his school and was enjoying his sports teams. Charles also continued to enjoy his job and the people he worked with. However, there had been some unforeseen changes. Charles told me the previous year that almost all hotels and resorts on the beach were for sale. The one he was managing had been up for sale for almost ten years with no results. And yet, less than nine months from the time he took over, it was sold. I always told him he did his job too well and made the place nice too quickly. It wasn't like it was a bargain of a deal, either, as the final sales price was more than $50 million. But the sale was now final, and our future was a little cloudier.

Having a resort that you manage get sold isn't always terrible. Sometimes it's just a new management company that takes over and you keep your job, so we hoped for that outcome. We had seen that scenario before, but we also experienced a job loss from this same situation in Texas. It was just the chance you take working in the hospitality industry. In this instance, however, Charles's resort was bought by a very well-known chain that we assumed would have their own people, especially for his position at the top. This was worrisome for us because we had no idea what we would do next. But as the transition to the new owners began, Charles seemed to be very much "in the loop" for their future plans. He was heavily involved in meetings for renovations and provided key information to the company about how this resort was successful and what ideas would work.

However, the new company was going to make some changes in the following weeks, and Charles was disheartened by them. Some long-term employees were going to lose their jobs because of cuts in the new budget. There was nothing he could do to stop it. Sometimes business is just business, and big companies don't get involved in personal matters. Firings are just another day at the office, even if those people have worked at a property for twenty years or are very good at their jobs. We would learn that lesson first-hand less than a month later.

Our morning went just like every other. We got Canyon ready for school and Charles was dressed for work. We said our goodbyes around 7:45 a.m., and Charles told me he had some meetings with the corporate staff of the new company. Unfortunately, they were letting another person go. It was going to be a difficult next few hours for him again.

When he walked back in the door at a little after 9 a.m., I remember casually saying, "Well that was quick. Are you taking the rest of the day off?"

"Yes," he replied. "The person they were letting go was me."

Unbelievable. After all he did for this new company to make their transition smooth and set them up for success, they had replaced him without a second thought and had planned to do so the whole time. There was a general manager from Atlanta who worked for the company, and he was just waiting for the news. He was not only waiting ready to step into the job, but also the house we were living in, as it was provided with the position. For our family of four, this was going to get complicated, and quickly.

So many employees told Charles in the previous weeks how they had interviews with this new company. When they had been questioned about him, they raved concerning the job Charles did and what a wonderful boss he was to work for. They spoke of how he turned this resort around, but apparently none of that mattered to the corporate leaders. In their eyes, he was expendable, like everyone else. Business was just business

146

to them, and money ruled their worlds. What did they care if we had a new baby and were a one-income household? They used Charles and got rid of him as soon as they had what they needed. It wasn't right, but we had experienced these types of unexplainable situations before with people going back on their word, and we knew there was no reason to dwell on it. There was no time to pout, just time to pray for another path and head on out again.

***

Life gets sticky, no doubt about it. What's crazy is we had been in difficult situations so many times it started to get easier to let the weight be taken off our shoulders. Each new twist made it crystal clear we were not in control, so why even attempt to take the reins? I'm not saying it made the situations easier to handle, but we knew to stop looking inward and lift our eyes upward.

> *Dear brothers and sisters, when troubles of any kind come your way, consider it an opportunity for great joy. For you know that when your faith is tested, your endurance has a chance to grow (James 1:2-3).*

CHAPTER 29

THE OPINION

NOVEMBER 2016, PENNSYLVANIA

After Mom's sudden cardiac death, the doctors told her she wasn't allowed to drive for three months because if the electrical issue was going to happen again, it would likely occur in that time span. That seemed like an eternity to her, so she was overjoyed when the last day of restriction arrived. Although she was retired, she was a very busy lady. It was difficult having to ask for a ride every time she wanted to go somewhere. She felt relieved her defibrillator never went off and she stopped worrying as much about it, because she was told her risk was very low at that point. But, it never hurts to have extra insurance, so the backup was still nice.

She was now back to much of normal life, aside from her shake schedule for her cancer. She was babysitting a few days a week and doing everything she normally did before her heart problem. I remember her telling me later that people were so amazed at how quickly she recovered and that she looked wonderful. I agreed; she did look fantastic! She felt great too; that was the best part of treating her cancer naturally, because she had no side effects. With all that product in her body, she was staying healthy and getting stronger week after week. She said she felt better than she had in twenty years.

Mom had two scans in the months prior to check the status of her cancer, and they didn't show much change. But at her last appointment, the oncologist was extremely pessimistic, and it would be our final appointment with him. I asked the doctor to take measurements to compare the latest scans because we wanted to see how much her tumor had decreased.

At first, he flat out refused and told us, "In my twenty-four years of experience, I can tell you what you are doing is never going to work."

We did not appreciate his negativity, especially regarding something he knew absolutely nothing about and hadn't taken any time to research. I have always respected different points of view, even if I don't agree with them, but not when someone is speaking without knowledge, and especially not when I could see how his gruffness was affecting my mom.

His attitude was even more frustrating because it was like many of the reactions Mom had faced since she started her treatment with the products. Few people thought it would work. She received lots and lots of "opinions" on how people thought she should best treat it. Most immediately recommended she have the surgery, because their sister or neighbor chose surgery and it worked out fine. I understood that advice and was happy for their positive results. If we had never learned of this life-changing nutrition, I am sure that is the route Mom would have also taken. Not treating cancer at all is not an option. Unless God performs a miracle on you, surely it will take your life eventually, and we knew that. So, people were just advising on what they knew, and it was traditional treatment. The bottom line was they cared about her, so she always did her best to hear them out.

Because most people don't know of other options, a high percentage choose surgery, but nobody ever talks about those who chose that option and later ended up with cancer in other parts of their body. The moment Mom got her diagnosis, I flew into research mode and learned all I could before I gave her my advice. I read accounts of cancer going into hiding during surgery only to reappear somewhere else or cells being left behind that later multiplied. I questioned Mom's oncologist on research about it spreading, but he had no answers for me. I wanted Mom to be fully informed when making her decisions, but apparently there were no research numbers that the doctor could give us for the negative outcomes of choosing traditional treatment. The doctor only gave statistics on what her five-year survival rate would be *with* surgery and radiation. I didn't want to hear anything about a five-year survival rate. My goal for her was to live the next thirty years with a wonderful quality of life. I know sometimes surgery and radiation is inevitable, and I respect whatever people decide is best for them. But for her, at this time, it didn't have to happen yet.

Some people did support her use of the nutrition but only in conjunction with traditional treatment. Very few gave their blessing for choosing the products alone. Our human nature is to be skeptical, but it was also difficult for Mom to hear that month after month from friends and family. People fear what they do not understand, and unfortunately 99 percent of these people did absolutely no research to learn more about what she was taking, so I understood her frustrations.

One acquaintance went so far as to tell her, "I'll see you at your funeral."

I thought that was a little over the top, but people can be crazy sometimes when they are being protective. Fear can make you say some questionable things. I suppose that was his way of showing he cared.

Mom's oncologist had his mind set strictly on getting her in for surgery and did not want any part of monitoring her progress with this nutrition. He told us the only reason he did the scan was to confirm the cancer was not growing. He was now confident it wasn't. This was where the consultation ended for him. It didn't take very long to realize that this patient/doctor relationship was not going to continue because this doctor was only interested in what he wanted and not what his patient wanted. I know there are many doctors out there who are very supportive of these supplements, mainly because they have taken the time to do the research. But, sometimes these situations do not work out, and it was time to find someone else. It was a disappointing appointment for Mom because she was being so positive about everything and so diligent in following her regimen. But, she quickly perked up when we left, as we made a new plan. She always told me she could handle anything if she had a plan. So, I was determined to get one in place as soon as possible. The best we could do was schedule a new scan at a different location three weeks later, but that just gave the products more time to work.

***

Although it is difficult to be around negativity, there was no reason to argue because I knew where Mom's healing would come from. Our God is awesome in power. He had proven it many times before, and I knew He would again.

> *What shall we say about such wonderful things as these?*
> *If God is for us, who can ever be [successful] against us?*
> *(Romans 8:31).*

CHAPTER 30

THE MOUNTAINS

AUGUST 2015, APPALACHIAN MOUNTAINS, VA

Charles and I missed living out west. I never had any intentions of moving there, but once I had the opportunity, I loved it. I would go back in a heartbeat, and so would he. However, as breathtaking as the scenery was it paled in comparison to the joy of seeing my mom's face. I relished watching her interact with my children, especially now that she was out of pain. So as Charles searched for a new job, he kept his options narrowed to the states around Pennsylvania, and I appreciated it immensely.

We were thrilled when he got an offer to manage a resort in the Appalachian Mountains of Virginia. It was as close to the feel of being out west as we could get and still be within four hours of the family. Move number 15 was about to begin. Although we were sad to leave our friends, we were going to be seven hours closer to my family and among the scenery we loved. Losing the job at the beach was looking like a blessing in disguise after all.

Canyon was becoming a pro at starting a new school. At nine, this was his fifth transfer. But I could see it making him more outgoing each time. Although change is difficult, especially for a child, it can have positive effects. I was proud of the way he was doing his best to embrace it. He quickly made new friends, and that winter he learned to ski for the first time and loved it. I thought he might miss the weather of South Carolina as well as the ocean, but he never did. Our children loved the snow, and we were going to have a lot of it.

CANCER ON MONDAY, DEAD ON TUESDAY, HOME BY THE WEEKEND

We were happy in Virginia for close to seven months when Charles came home from work one day and said, "I got a call today."

There were so many directions this conversation could go—good, bad, or neutral. I almost didn't want to ask more details. But I did. He told me he received a call from a resort in Pennsylvania. He had applied to just about every resort job opening ever posted in Pennsylvania through the years, but the opportunities were rare. For the last eight years, he had always kept his eye open for a position because he was still trying to make good on his promise to my mom to bring me home. But, nothing ever looked very promising. Although it is a large state for the east coast, there are very few areas that have resorts besides the Poconos, and even in that vacation spot jobs are hard to come by. Everyone wants one, so the competition is fierce. Since we moved to Virginia, Charles had stopped searching for the first time. We enjoyed this area and felt blessed to be this close to the family. We were content.

"Did you apply to this resort?" I asked.

"No," he said. "I can only guess they got my name from a recruiter. I don't really know."

The resort was in the northern part of the Poconos and its name sounded familiar. When he showed it to me online, I remembered immediately. On our one year anniversary, we were living in Pennsylvania and wanted a fun place to spend the weekend. We stayed at the resort he was talking about. It was all-inclusive and had lots of sports and activities that had been perfect for us. What a crazy coincidence.

"Well, what did they want?" I prodded.

"They want me to drive up for an interview," he said.

Now, this was all coming at me a little too fast. All I wanted the last several years was to get back close to my family, but I had let that go in the past months and really focused on making a life in Virginia. I had recently made new friends and was connecting with people to grow my business. I joined a basketball league that winter for the first time in many years and had a great time playing again. Maverick and I had a daily routine of walking up and down the mountain we lived on and we loved the views. I was very comfortable.

I was also having trouble wrapping my head around how this all came about. He didn't apply for this job but they called him out of the blue, and after one phone conversation wanted to do an on-site interview? It didn't seem real. It was fantastic but also overwhelming. As much as I wanted to entertain the idea, no part of me wanted to think about moving again. I loved our house and had just set it up the way I wanted. And what in the world would we do if he got this job? The Poconos area is remote and there aren't a lot of rentals, and if this were to be the area where we raised our kids then shouldn't we just buy a house? But how in the world were we going to make that happen? When would we even have a chance to look? We also still had a lease on this rental home. This was a logistical nightmare in my mind, and he didn't even have a job offer yet.

After years of moving, this was the way my brain worked—I would look five steps ahead when a new job prospect was presented. Charles took a few minutes to get me thinking calmly again and helped me look at the positives. We would be within two hours of the family and could attend all special occasions. We could purchase our own farm— something we always promised Canyon we would do if it was possible. The kids could have great relationships with their cousins and make lasting memories with everyone else. They would not miss out on things like they did when we lived farther away. I couldn't believe this could really be a possibility.

Two weeks later, I had to tell our landlord we were breaking our lease and leaving at the end of the month. It had to be at least the fourth time we had done this over the years. The logistical nightmare had worked itself out in an unbelievable way and at warp speed. The weekend after Charles was offered the job, we dropped the kids off at Mom's and spent eight hours looking at homes.

We couldn't find anything we liked. As we were on the way to the very last possibility, Charles said to our realtor, "I remember there was one house you emailed us about that Tricia said she didn't want to see, but I liked it. Is it still available?"

"Yes, and it's actually on the way to this final home we are headed to," he said.

You could just chalk that up to luck, but if you saw the amount of driving we did that day looking for houses, it was incredible. There was always at least twenty to thirty minutes of searching in different directions for each new home on our list, and we were exhausted. When we reached Charles's pick, we could only pull into the driveway because we didn't have an appointment.

Charles immediately looked at me and said, "That's it."

Well. He didn't have me sold yet, because we still had the house that was my favorite from our online search coming up. But, five minutes after viewing the home that was my "favorite," our agent was on the phone making an appointment for the house Charles liked. The final home on our original list was next to what looked like a junkyard, so it was scratched immediately. Beautiful home, terrible location, and not meant to be.

We got into a multiple-offer bidding war, but one week later we had it. The home our children would grow up in. After seeing it in person, it just felt right. We both knew it from the moment we got out of the car. On May 1, 2016, we were officially Pennsylvania residents again. And what seemed like misfortune in losing a job nine months before had turned out to be one of our greatest gains. It was what we prayed for all along. We were coming "home," and Charles made good on his promise with a lot of help from up above.

> I look up to the mountains—does my help come from there?
> My help comes from the Lord, who made heaven and earth!
> (Psalms 121:1-2)

CHAPTER 31

THE NEWS

My phone rang a little after 7 p.m., and it was my mom. We small talked for a few minutes, and then she let me know she had something to tell me, and it was no big deal. We could read each other like a book, so we always tried to set the stage when there was no reason to worry. She had just left her family doctor, but everything was fine, she assured me.

Earlier that day, she had felt light-headed and passed out. She had a few seconds warning, and thankfully did not hit her head on anything on the way down. She guessed she was unconscious only for a minute or two, and when she woke up, she felt totally normal. Usually, I would have gotten a phone call right away, but Mom was hesitant to tell anyone, even Dave, so she kept quiet about it all day. She didn't want anyone getting upset if it was no big deal. Thankfully, she decided to make an appointment to see her doctor that night. She finally told Dave on her way out the door, and he went with her. After explaining the details of the event and having a few tests run, her doctor assumed it was an issue with her blood pressure medicine. Her numbers were still a bit high, so she had recently started a new pill. He told her that sometimes if it's too high a dose, you can pass out. He said to cut her pills in half and, just to be on the safe side, call the hospital that put her defibrillator in and tell them what happened. The defibrillator kept a record of her daily heart rhythms, so she left a message to ask them to check the timing of when she passed out. Her call to the hospital was on Friday. I didn't like hearing she passed out, but it sounded like it wasn't a problem, and the doctor had a plan to keep it from happening again. I was relieved.

On Tuesday morning when my phone rang again, there was no small talk, and I knew Mom was upset within moments. Through her tears, she told me the hospital called her back with news about her event. She didn't just pass out; her heart had stopped again. Remember how I said earlier I hoped lightning would not strike her twice? Well, it did. The defibrillator kicked in and restarted her heart and that's why she woke back up. I had no words. Usually I go right into my positive response for why something bad happens—a habit I learned from my mom. I will lay out a plan on all the ways we will make things better and that it's okay. This time, I started to bawl. I am sure this was not the soothing comfort she was looking for, but I had nothing.

"They took my license away again, Tricia! And indefinitely this time," she sobbed. "Do you know what that is going to do to an independent person like me? I never understood why they talked about depression in the defibrillator packet. I never saw any reason to be depressed, but now I get it. Look at what is happening to me. I feel great and yet I have died—twice. They say it could happen again at any time. I can't live like that."

Everything she was saying made sense. She was extremely grateful to be saved a second time, but how would it feel to be confined to your home while wondering if your heart was going to stop at any minute? I had no answers for her, but I also had to be honest. I told her I was sorry she felt that way but I couldn't be anything but thankful she was still alive. Two times I should have lost her and yet we were on the phone. She was alone this time when her heart stopped, and if she didn't have that defibrillator she would have died. After I settled down, I did my best to comfort her and let her know everything was going to fine, even though I didn't know if that was true. It was all so hard to comprehend.

At her cardiologist appointment the next week, the doctor confirmed our fears that she was a walking time bomb and that it could happen again at any moment. The doctor informed her that one of these times the defibrillator was not going to bring her back. Well, if she wasn't depressed before, she was going to have to fight hard to stay positive now. That was terrible news and more than frightening. Why did God bring her back so miraculously if He was just going to allow her to die from something so uncontrollable? Especially when she was still fighting her cancer and wanting so much to bring hope to others for this natural treatment. Mom, Dave, and I talked many times about how she was going to change lives and be an inspiration. I knew that to be true, but we had not yet gotten a chance to prove it.

I was frightened for her future and I knew she was too. To my knees was the only place I could go, and I did. We needed God's hand on her body every second, and I sent my prayers continuously. She needed protection until doctors figured out how to help her.

She wore a heart monitor that weekend, and her doctor said she had 300 extra beats a day. It was those beats that were so dangerous. She was not a candidate for surgery, so the only option was medication. There was a chance it could work in a few weeks, so she began it immediately and set an appointment for December to follow up. We could only pray the doctors knew what they were doing and that God would heal her through their knowledge.

The next few weeks were excruciating, waiting for her cancer scan while trying to deal with her unresolved heart issue. I felt a huge weight because I knew she needed good news. I explained to her in the beginning that everyone's body is different, and you couldn't put a timetable on how long it would take for her immune system to flush out the cancer. I knew stories of people who were cancer-free in six weeks, but I also knew stories of it taking six months or longer, so there was no definitive answer, although she wanted one. With how difficult these past weeks had been on her soul, there was nothing more I wanted than for her to be able to celebrate.

As I got in the car that Wednesday morning to drive to her house in order to go with her and Dave to the appointment, I thought of where this journey began. Sometimes it felt like a movie that was playing in slow motion, and it was as if I was watching it from the outside. But the pain was real, and we all felt it. Her death was all too real and I still had trouble even thinking about it at times. This woman was my world; I needed her and so did everyone else. This cancer *had* to be gone.

***

Mom's cardiologist would later tell her she was the luckiest unlucky person he had ever met. Yes, she died twice, and yet she was alive. How many people get that many chances? I certainly didn't believe it was luck, but it was still scary regardless. My heart was full of gratefulness, but these past few months were a gut-wrenching experience. So it was back to basics—knees on the ground, hands folded, head bowed. Help her, dear God, she needs You.

> *I will call to you whenever I'm in trouble, and you will answer me (Psalms 86:7).*

CHAPTER 32

THE MEMORIES

MAY 2016, THE POCONOS, PA

Moving into our new home was the best change we could ask for. The kids had not seen the house, so watching them explore the place where they would make memories for years to come was amazing. Canyon and Charles began to make plans for animals in the back and talked of what we would get and where the barn would go. In the next few weeks, I watched Canyon embrace farm life. He went out each weekend with Charles to clear land for the animals and worked longer hours than I'd ever seen before.

We had a large paved driveway for the first time and a spacious yard, so we had a great time playing basketball and throwing a football, and Maverick toddled everywhere. My mom came over to help me arrange the house as always. It was so cool that she could just hop in the car and not have to fly. We were going to have so many amazing times in this house, and I looked forward to sharing it all with her. We lived in some unbelievable places through the years, and I would not change any of them for the world, but it is always more special to have everyone you love share in memories with you. She was a key to it all.

As summer began, we got into a routine at the new house and had some new additions. Our little farm now had two miniature donkeys and six goats. They were a lot of work but worth every second, and watching Canyon interact with them was priceless. I could see he had an innate way with animals just like his father. My brother Justin's family came over to visit one weekend, and it was just as I always pictured. I watched from the front porch as the kids made up games and ran through the yard, having a blast. Family—it's what life is all about, and we were all together.

As the sun began its descent and I continued to watch the kids play until it got dark, I thanked God for the path He set for us. It was hard to believe we were here. From the time we met, Charles and I lived in ten states, moved into twenty different homes and finally came full circle with our two children. We always asked Canyon—if he could live anywhere, where would he choose? Pennsylvania was his answer every time, and this was coming from a child who lived at the Grand Canyon, Lake Powell, Arizona, and Myrtle Beach. "Why?" we always asked him.

"My family," was his consistent reply.

"Me too," I would tell him.

***

I could have never foreseen how close we would come to having the whole concept of family be torn apart less than a month later. I think that's why the call at 6:19 a.m. on June 28, 2016 was so earth-shattering for me. In all the years I was away, Mom and I immediately planned our next visit the moment we had to leave each other. We always wanted confirmation of the next time we would meet, so the distance didn't hurt so badly. That phone call was a startling reality of the possibility of never making that plan again. I lived so close now, I was making plans more than ever, so excited for the future. A future that on that day, I didn't know if she would live to see. I will never be able to thank God enough for the way He saved her. There was no luck, there were no coincidences; God saved her. Yes, He used people to make it happen as He often does, but His timing was perfect, as always, and no man could have orchestrated all that He did on that day.

> *I am leaving you with a gift—peace of mind and heart. And the peace I give is a gift the world cannot give. So don't be troubled or afraid (John 14:27).*

CHAPTER 33

THE RESULTS

NOVEMBER 30ᵗʰ 2016, PENNSYLVANIA

Mom, Dave, and I all drove together to a nearby town for the cancer scan.

"I'm nervous," Mom admitted.

I was a little also, but did my best to remain calm. We were going to know one way or another in about half an hour. I wasn't going to be discouraged if the cancer was still there, but I knew she would. She really deserved some good news. I prayed she would get it.

As we drove we talked about another blessing from Mom's story that came at just the right time and was completely unexpected. One day in July, Mom had called me and said a man Dave worked with was going to be renting one of their bedrooms upstairs. I did my best not to say anything negative, but I didn't like this idea. The more she told me about it, the more I learned that Dave didn't really know this man all that well but just had a good feeling about him. That detail made me even less comfortable with this living situation. The man was working on a job site that took him four hours from his family, and during the week he needed a place to stay. Recently, he was staying at a hotel, but he wasn't happy there. After some prayer, Dave felt led to offer him a room in their house. His co-worker was very grateful and moved in the next week.

There was an awkward silence between the three of them the day he arrived regarding how much he would pay in rent, because Mom and

Dave had no experience in renting out a room. Finally, Mom threw out a number. The man countered by offering an extra $100 a month for lights and electricity, which was very thoughtful. He turned out to be the most wonderful renter they could ask for. He was very kind, along with being extremely neat, and most times it was like he wasn't even there. Why was this such a cool part of the story? Because the extra product Mom was buying each month to fight her cancer with was a strain on their budget. The amount of money they received from rent was the exact amount they needed to cover her nutritional supplements. It was just enough with that extra $100 he had added of his own free will. As we pulled up to the building, Mom let me know that the man just moved out the week prior.

"Wouldn't it be amazing if he moved out the exact month your cancer is gone, and you don't need that money to buy extra products this month?" I asked.

"Yes, that would be perfect," Mom replied.

In a short amount of time, we would know if this scenario would be true.

Before we got out of the car, Dave wanted to say a prayer. He asked God to reveal Himself to us and continue to have His hand on Mom through this journey. He prayed God's will be done on this day. As we walked into the building together, we were ready for His answer.

I went into the room with Mom for the scan. There were many audible breaths taken as she sat down and got into the proper position. The tension was almost palpable. As much as we put our trust in God, human nature tries to take over and I knew Mom was working hard to stay calm. I could tell she wanted to be able to read the result as it was happening. She continuously strained her neck to look at the screen, but it was no use; she was just going to have to be patient. Even if she could have seen it, neither of us had any idea what we were looking at. The whole process was over in twenty minutes. After months of preparation and commitment to the plan, along with prayer without ceasing, less than a half hour was all it took to see if she had been restored to health. As she got dressed, Dave came in to hear the results. When Mom reentered the room, the three of us gathered together to hear the outcome. The room felt devoid of air. You could hear a pin drop as we waited anxiously. I think we were collectively holding our breath while praying fervently to God.

Thankfully, the doctor's personality put us more at ease when she introduced herself and sat down to talk. She was supportive of Mom's choices and made us feel comfortable immediately because of her easygoing nature.

She looked at the scan thoroughly and pointed to the area of concern. As she turned her chair back around to face us her expression lightened.

"I see *nothing*," she said.

This announcement was met with silence. None of us moved, no one exhaled, and no one said a word. After the most difficult few months we had all endured as a family, this was exactly what we wanted to hear. Yet not one of us reacted. We just looked at each other wide eyed and mute. No whoops or hollers or celebrations, which is rare for Mom and me because we are very demonstrative and are likely to burst into song over the smallest delight. Dave is more laid back, so I understood him being quiet. I think it's just that we were stunned. Yes, we believed in these products and knew what they could do and how God would heal her through them. We saw the science and the powerful testimonies of others. But now we were experiencing it firsthand with a deadly disease like cancer, a disease that kills thousands upon thousands of people every year—people who were fighting just as hard as my mom to survive. All three of us knew of friends who lost a mother or a brother or a child. But here we were, standing together with a woman who had not only died twice but now had been healed of a life-threatening condition in less than five months and without medical treatment. We were in silent awe for quite a while and listened intently as the doctor explained the results in more detail.

"If I didn't know you had cancer previously, I would have said you were perfectly healthy looking at this scan. It's totally clear."

Simply amazing.

I think our response to the results was a culmination of the journey, of the weight that had piled on everyone's shoulders—especially Mom's. But it had all been worth it. A few moments later, I finally saw a smile began to spread on Mom's face, and I returned the grin. You see could her feel like she could take a deep, cleansing breath after this arduous journey. I watched as she slowly let her shoulders rise up and then release. Maybe we just weren't sure if we could celebrate because this was all new territory for us. We thanked everyone profusely and headed for the door. Once outside I lifted my head to the sky in acknowledgment of God's glory. As I felt my familiar personality return, I took a moment to gather myself.

I quickly allowed the joy to rush into my body in response to yet another miracle and shouted, "Her boob is clear! Her boob is clear!"

This got a cackle from my mom. Her cackle is one of the most joyous sounds on earth for me. Because of how God's hands were on both our lives and the way He brought her back from the dead and led me to an answer that would heal her, I was now going to get to hear that laugh for years to come.

I give God all the glory for her healing. Just as I said earlier, sometimes He uses people to do His will, and I also believe He firmly has His hands on these products in the same way and put them in my path. As we drove home, I realized something that had slipped my mind while I was so focused on this appointment. The day was November 30, my niece's second birthday. My mom got her amazing news on a day we celebrated the birth of her only granddaughter, a child with the middle name Faith. What a time for celebration! What a wonderful reminder in the years to come to relish life on this day for more than one reason.

There was more good news a few weeks later. On December 19, Mom returned to the cardiologist for a check on her heart. There were still some extra beats, but things had improved enough that she was again allowed to drive. Her medication was increased to speed up the process of eliminating the remaining extra beats, but the doctor said with each day she lessened her chances of reoccurrence. And yet there are no guarantees. The events of the past six months showed us that first-hand. We must have faith that God will provide. He had provided in a big way, and we believed He would continue to do so going forward. Life is a gift every day, and we need to cherish the time God gives us. I am so grateful He gave us more time with my mom, and I know His plans for her are limitless. He is not finished with her yet—not by a long shot.

Mom and I have always had a bond that is unbreakable. We have taken very different paths in our lives. But I now realize that even when we were separated by thousands of miles at different times, God always led us back to each other, weaving our stories together as only He could. Fifteen years after I first left her for Colorado, we are now separated by less than one hundred miles. Through that journey across the country, God put me just where I needed to be, and it had phenomenal results for us and our whole family. My life would never be the same without my mom and had she died from her heart issue or her cancer, a part of me would have died along with her. Ultimately, He saved us both.

I admit there were times I questioned God and felt angry at the things that were happening to Mom and my family. But all the while He was carrying us, we were never alone. He continued to pave the way for our paths to meet again. Through it all He showed me He was always in control, and it was all for His glory. My mom is alive and well. She will change lives with her story—I am sure of it. She is a light in this world and always has been. And her light will only continue to shine brighter with each passing day.

I think next year on Black Friday, Mom and I are going to have to venture out again to shop and spread some more of her joy. So, if you're standing in a huge line, becoming frustrated at your wait, and hear the worst version of "Jingle Bells" ever sung, say a prayer and thank God for His perfect timing. Because that ear-piercing sound is coming from living proof of a miracle who is just trying to spread a little *"Christmas cheer!"*

***

Sickness. Death. Tragedy. Despair. These things affect each and every one of us throughout our lives; no one is exempt from pain. In our journey here on earth, sometimes we experience a complete loss of hope. I have been there; my whole family has felt the weight of the world. I think back to that time outside of the hospital when I was crumpled in a heap on the ground at the thought of my mom dying. Or feeling a knife in the heart when I knew we had lost a fourth child, another precious and innocent life. But there is hope in the storm.

Living through all of our family's difficulties, I now know something that I couldn't say I was certain of until this past year. The greatest faith is born in the hour of despair. When I saw no way out, my faith rose like never before, and it was that faith that brought victory. When you are at your lowest, cry out to Jesus. He will answer you and create beauty from the ashes.

***

"'For I know the plans I have for you,' says the Lord. 'They are plans for good and not for disaster, to give you a future and a hope'" (Jeremiah 29:11).

For More Information

If you would like to learn more about the nutritional supplements mentioned throughout the book, you can email Tricia at triciakingcontact@gmail.com. They are not sold on store shelves. You can also view some of the reality of what has happened to others at her Facebook page, *Mission: Optimal Family Nutrition,* and message her there. This nutrition is not specific to only cancer. The body is the miracle and knows what to do when you give it the proper fuel. This page will give testimonials on many different issues, along with the prevention of disease. She also has a website for more information where you can contact her at www.king.reliv.com.

Statements on these products have not been evaluated by the Food and Drug Administration. They are not intended to diagnose, treat, cure or prevent any disease.

About the Author

TRICIA KING is a health and wellness coach. She studied at St. Bonaventure University in New York, receiving a BA in Elementary Education/Writing while playing Division 1 basketball. She has traveled extensively in the United States, living in eleven different states from east to west. After seeing the needs of so many in her travels, she is passionate about helping more people achieve health and prevention through natural options.

Tricia can be contacted at triciakingcontact@gmail.com.

We are a Christian-based publishing company that was founded in 2009. Our primary focus has been to establish authors.

"5 Fold Media was the launching partner that I needed to bring *The Transformed Life* into reality. This team worked diligently and with integrity to help me bring my words and vision into manifestation through a book that I am proud of and continues to help people and churches around the world. None of this would have been possible without the partnership and education I received from 5 Fold Media."

- Pastor John Carter, Lead Pastor of Abundant Life Christian Center, Syracuse, NY, Author and Fox News Contributor

The Transformed Life is foreworded by Pastor A.R. Bernard, received endorsements from best-selling authors Phil Cooke, Rick Renner, and Tony Cooke, and has been featured on television shows such as TBN and local networks.

5 Fold Media
315.570.3333 | 5701 E. Circle Dr. #338, Cicero, NY 13039
manuscript@5foldmedia.com

Find us on Facebook, Twitter, and YouTube

Discover more at www.5FoldMedia.com.

Capturing the Supernatural

Are you ready to experience healing right here, right now?

Most of us believe (or want to believe) that God still shows up in miraculous ways—that He supernaturally intervenes in our lives. But how come it always seems to happen to someone else, often in some far-away place? This book will uplift and inspire you to believe not only that divine healing happens today, but that it's happening far more often than you might imagine.

As you read these well-documented stories of supernatural healing you will find your faith growing. Along the way you will gain fresh insight and instruction on key principles that may play a role in you receiving your healing.

"My heart was refreshed and my spirit was stirred as I read *Healed!: Present Day Stories of Healing and How it Happens*, by my dear friends Andy and Cathy Sanders. This is a timely message for the bride of Christ! I believe that the reader will not only experience God's healing power, but they will also find that they are living at a new level of faith. This book truly captures the supernatural. It's destined to be a classic!"

— **Patrick Schatzline, Founder of Remnant Ministries International** Author of *Why Is God So Mad at Me?*; *I Am Remnant*; and *Unqualified: Where You Can Begin to be Great*. www.iamremnant.me

Get ready to be encouraged and blessed as you read these candid, unfiltered accounts of supernatural healings.

Visit www.capturingthesupernatural.com for more information.

CPSIA information can be obtained
at www.ICGtesting.com
Printed in the USA
BVOW06s1130051117
499597BV00019B/552/P

9 781942 056546